HOW TO GROW A MONEYTREE

HOW TO GROW A MONEYTREE!

The Magical Book of Making Big Money With Second Mortgages

Dave Glubetich

REALTOR

ISBN 0-9601 530-0-4

THE MONOPOLY GAME
and
HOW TO GROW A MONEYTREE
are available for $9.95 each
from
Glubetich Enterprises
12 Gregory Lane
Pleasant Hill, Calif. 94523
(415) 689-5090

To Janet, with love

Acknowledgments

Moneytree would not be a reality today if it wasn't for the wonderful encouragement, help and support that I received from so many friends and co-workers. To the following I express my deep gratitude: Janet Glubetich, a great typist . . . . . Gene Kenworthy and Lou Shuman, two very knowledgeable loan brokers . . . . . Richard Smith, Bob Joy and Hank Lasiter, three title company "experts" . . . . . Judy Maddy and Joan Gardner, who made so many "research" telephone calls . . . . . Art Hawkins, a real whiz with figures . . . . . Dave and Janet Williams, very capable text readers . . . . . Lon Carlston, an invaluable help with editing . . . . . Mildred Goodman, a great "idea" gal . . . . . and certainly the staff at Wells Realty who have been so patient and understanding for such a long time.

Contents

APPENDIX

courtesy of First American Title Insurance Company

Introduction

When I was a boy, I could never understand why my father never had enough money. After all, he had a good paying job. He must have been earning close to $600 a month in those days.

By the time I was a senior at Oakland Tech High School, I was a lot smarter. But I was still perplexed. I had discovered that my father's income was better than the national average. But why then were we still so broke?

Like a lot of America's youth, I needed to get married before I would start to realize what happens to money. I soon discovered that the answer was really quite simple and a little frightening. Most of the money I earned would go for things I really didn't want to spend it on. Like BILLS — medical, grocery, insurance, etc. which can just about eat up most salaries. And TAXES which certainly take care of what may or may not be left of your income. And last but not least, INFLATION which for most people is the demon that sinks the ship.

Years later I learned not only how to cope with these problems but how to actually stay ahead of the game of life. Again the answer was quite simple. I had to invest. And I found the best investments to be real property (for tax shelter and rapid equity growth) and second mortgages which could help me safely accumulate large sums of money at returns well above the rate of inflation.

It took me a long time to learn. I hope this book can shorten that process for you.

"Moneytree" is about people and money. People helping people in ways that benefit both parties — lender and borrower — investor and homeowner.

Unknown by many investors, the world of second mortgages is an exciting and profitable investment field that is tailor-made for the creative do-it-yourself person.

The subject of second mortgages and deeds of trust need not be told in dry, text book style. To be sure there are complicated phases, technical procedures and state laws to familiarize yourself with. But I think you will be surprised at how simple it actually is, because second investing is really a people to people business. Before you lies less than 120 pages of easy to understand explanations of what at the onset may seem like a terribly complicated subject. But it really isn't!

Literally thousands of people—from all walks of life—are currently earning 9 to 12 per cent yearly on their money. And they are doing this without lifting a finger and without any serious risk to their money. Others are earning 15 to 30 per cent with hardly any more knowledge or effort than those earning 9 and 12 per cent.

The beauty of a second investment program is that you have a choice of several different directions. You can sit back and let a competent loan broker handle your portfolio or you can become fully involved and originate your own loans. If you are a good horse trader you can buy seconds for an excellent profit.

"Moneytree" will also help the non-investor who needs to "carry back" a loan to make the sale on his own property. He will learn that his "purchase money" second isn't a liability after all but just may be a safe and sound way to make extra money.

Although I often stress the "safety" of second investments, there are some pitfalls to be aware of. Part of the purpose of this book is to stress the right way to create, buy and sell your seconds. When you follow the relatively easy and basic rules of the trade, then and only then will your investments be "safe and sound."

To fully understand the proper procedures, you must know your state laws with respect to second mortgages or trust deeds, maximum interest rates, foreclosures, loan brokers, etc. Much of this information will be covered in this book. But remember that even though there are many similarities and standardizations, the laws of the 50 states do vary. What's legal in Kentucky probably is legal in Oregon. But a fine difference in the law could cost you money, so be safe and check it out.

I am sure that you will find "Moneytree" just a little bit magical with the many ways it shows you how to make a greater profit with your investment dollar. By following many of the suggestions in this book you can create a tidy sum of money in just a few years. You can start with as little as $2,000 or as much as you care to. Whatever amount you put into your investment program, you can be sure of one thing, it's going to grow.

Good reading and a long and prosperous retirement!

I

Making Money
With Seconds

Welcome to the world of moneylenders! Now don't be alarmed when I tell you that you've already been lending your money—and to total strangers at that.

For instance, the money you deposit in your checking account is used by your bank so it can profit on it by making loans. Of course we're talking about millions of dollars and millions of people. And your bank is regulated so that it can't lend all your money—so you will never have to worry about one of your checks not being covered. In small ways you get paid for this service. Like a free checking account with a minimum $100 balance.

The circulation and flow of money—often arranged by money-lenders—is what keeps the world economy going. There are people who have legitimate reasons to lend their capital and there are people who have legitimate reasons to borrow. Many needs are on a small scale.

This is where the "second" moneylender comes into the picture. When a family is knee deep in debt and the bank and credit union have to turn him away—where does he go? If he is a home-owner he can turn to secondary financing. You've heard it advertised as debt consolidation loans for homeowners.

The principle is simple. If Mr. & Mrs. Borrower owe department stores a total of $5,000 with combined monthly payments of $400, you might say their budget is being stretched. If they are homeowners with a fair amount of equity in their property, they can borrow the $5,000 and pay less than $110 a month for five years. And this new loan will probably be at 8 to 12 per cent interest—not the 18 per cent so common for department store revolving account "service charges."

The above example is only one of hundreds of legitimate reasons people have for borrowing. To this list you could add the investor who is seeking better leverage; a widowed mother putting a son through college; a growing family remodeling its present home; the family taking a well deserved vacation. The list of those needing the moneylender's services goes on and on.

The reasons people invest money may be as numerous as the reasons people borrow. One important reason is future retirement because that is something we all look forward to. Other good reasons would include a current need for extra income or a desire to build a secure estate.

The only real difference that separates most borrowers from most moneylenders is that the lender is probably thinking ahead more than the borrower. He is planning today for tomorrow's college education.

WHAT ARE SECONDS?

Secondary financing can be simply defined as a loan secured by a second mortgage or deed of trust on real property. We'll take a closer look at the technical aspects of seconds later in the book. But for now the key point to remember is that seconds are ONLY secured by real property.

Loans secured by automobiles, televisions, promissory notes or just plain good faith are not part of this book. They are often risky and take a special kind of expertise.

As a "second moneylender" you are interested only in the legal homeowner of record with a "safe" amount of equity in his property. The money that you lend him, secured by both a promissory note and a second deed of trust or mortgage, can be as safe as money in the bank. Only your second investment will pay you much bigger dividends than will the bank.

INVESTMENT CHOICES

In addition to "second" investing, there are other fields which attract a lot of investment dollars from the great American middle-class. They must be compared keeping in mind the U.S. Labor Department's Consumer Price Index.

The CPI (also known as the Cost-of-Living-Index) reflects the changes in the cost of goods and services to a typical consumer, based on the costs of the same goods and services at a base period.

Currently using 1967 as a base year, the CPI has risen from 100.00 in 1967 to 161.2 at the end of 1975. This means that inflation has risen by an average annual rate of 6.8 per cent over the past nine years.

The man that buries his money in a tin can will lose an average of 6.8 cents on each dollar each year. Inflation will definitely get the best of him.

Almost everyone can understand how the man who buries his money will lose out. But surprisingly some people can't understand why the savings account investor who earns all of 4½ to 5½ per cent annually on his money is also a big loser. Even at 5½ per cent this investor is losing 1.3 cents on each dollar to inflation. If your investment cannot put you on a road that earns you more money than the cost of living index takes from you—then you are kidding yourself—YOU ARE NOT INVESTING YOUR MONEY.

LET'S EXAMINE A FEW OTHER POPULAR INVESTMENT ALTERNATIVES:

Stock Market: Anyone who has invested in a broad range of stocks over the past few years has probably lost money. The stock market has many peaks and valleys and it takes a wise and well schooled investor to buy low and sell high accurately enough to make a consistent profit. For most people it represents a pure gamble similar to one you would make on the tables of Las Vegas.

In addition, even the best dividend-paying stocks only return 6 to 8 per cent on your dollar. And in many cases these dividends are not guaranteed.

A friend retired with several thousand dollars invested in high dividend stocks. The portfolio was carefully chosen to give him a good retirement income. But in the slump of 1974 the bottom fell out! His income — as well as the stock values — was cut down next to nothing. Even at this writing his projected income is still not what he thought it was going to be prior to 1974.

Bonds: Triple A rated corporate bonds can pay upwards to 8 per cent interest. But this is a taxable income. Municipal bonds can offer a tax-free investment, but these bonds will pay only 3 to 7 per cent. And to realize the top interest rates you must have triple A rated bonds and hold them to a maturity of up to 30 years.

According to a friend who sells bonds, "no one buys municipal bonds to make money, but they are good investments for those in the 50 per cent and higher tax brackets."

Gold: "All that glitters is not gold," and sometimes not even gold. The glamorous gold market became legal for U.S. citizens on Jan. 1, 1975. At that time the price of gold was $186 per ounce and expected to go higher. On October 7, 1976 the price of gold was $115. And remember—gold pays no interest or dividends.

Life Insurance: I am not going to argue against the premise that a man or woman needs life insurance to protect their family in case of an untimely death. However, I think it is ridiculous that life insurance (mutual whole life programs) are sold as an investment or even as a source of retirement income. The reason is simple—your profit is in the form of dividends which historically pay only 5 to 6 per cent per year.

Savings Accounts: Billions of American dollars are in banks or savings and loan accounts. They are earning from 4½ to as high as 8 per cent in time certificate accounts, which have penalties for early withdrawals. (Remember, though, if you haven't been earning more than 6.8 per cent these past nine years you are really losing money.)

Of course, you say, these savings accounts are insured by an agency of the federal government. But I think many of you will be surprised later on when you see how "seconds" are an almost fail-safe investment.

Income Property: Here's a good investment for not only tax shelter but fantastic equity growth. And I sincerely believe that single family homes for most people of middle income means is by far and away the best thing going. In my book "The Monopoly Game, the how to book of making big money with rental homes," I show how it is possible to make up to 100 per cent return per year on many investments.

But even though homes (or larger apartments) can be unbelievably profitable, there is an element of risk and a lot of "work" to be done. Owning just two or three properties can be fun and not take up too much time. But as an investor begins to approach 10 to 15 homes, he finds himself saddled with a part-time job. And for anyone who is looking forward to a peaceful and rewarding retirement, 10 or 15 properties may be a little too much.

Seconds: Second deeds of trust (mortgages) are relatively easy to acquire and to manage. But best of all they are a safe investment that can pay anywhere from a minimum of 10 per cent interest to a high return of even 25 per cent.

With seconds there are a lot of different directions you can go. You can take on the whole project yourself or you can "hire" a competent mortgage broker. And if you live in a state with low legal contract interest rates — don't be discouraged because you too can earn upwards to 25 per cent.

Seconds for profit is what "Moneytree" is all about. As you read on I am convinced you will become a believer in the opportunities that exist for this type of investment.

ESTABLISH YOUR "FINANCIAL GOAL"

One potential problem with "seconds" is that you will be presented with monthly opportunities to "reach into the cookie jar." While this is what the retiree is looking for, it can be very damaging to the investor looking for financial independence 20 or 30 years down the road.

Because of the nature of "second" investing, you must be prepared to exercise a reasonable amount of self-discipline and to establish a realistic personal goal. Without a sense of direction you will find yourself getting nowhere fast. You must set your sights on a goal and do everything in your power to reach it.

You must create a "financial goal" for a specific net worth or income after a pre-determined amount of years. Your goal must be believable, worthwhile and obtainable. It must also fit your personality and future income needs.

If your goal isn't believable, you probably won't even get started with your program. If it isn't worthwhile, you will lose interest along the way. If it isn't obtainable, you will become discouraged and give up. If it doesn't match your personality (conservative and slower approach for a conservative person vs. a more aggressive approach) you will bog down and have to start over again.

In order to determine what your financial goal should be, it is necessary to develop a current and future budget. Your current budget will tell you where you stand now and how much money you can afford to put into your investment program.

Your future budget should be an estimate of your needs and expenses at the time you want to be financially independent. And by financially independent I mean that time in your life when you don't need to work anymore. When you will be able to live off the earnings of your investments, coupled with any other retirement benefits you may be getting.

In order to establish your future expenses, go through your current budget item by item and try to visualize the changes which may occur in your living style. Determine where you will need more or less income. To avoid complications at this point, assume that the purchasing power of the dollar remains the same.

After you finish your "financial independence" budget there is one important step to take. It is more than probable that the inflationary trend of the U.S. economy will continue. In fact over the past nine years this figure has averaged 6.8 per cent per year, as I mentioned earlier. This means that a dollar today may be worth only about 50 cents in 15 years at the current trend. Thus, if your future budget calls for an income of $2,000 per month you will really need $4,000 over a 15-year span.

To determine your future needs, refer to the "Inflation Factor Table" on page 97. This table, with annual inflation rates ranging from 3 to 7.5 per cent, allows you to work with the rate you believe most likely to happen.

To determine your adjusted income requirements, select a rate of inflation and match it with the number of years left before your financial independence. For example, if you have estimated inflation at 6 per cent and you have a 30-year financial goal, then your factor would be 5.743.

Your next step is to multiply your "factor" by your required annual income prior to inflation adjustment. Thus in our example, if your income figure was $15,000, you would multiply 15,000 x 5.743 to get $86,145.

Many readers may be in a state of shock at this pont. But the facts are simple—if inflation continues at 6 per cent (which is even lower than the actual 6.8 per cent of the past nine years) you will need $86,145 in 30 years to match the $15,000 income that gets you by today. The moral of this example is also simple—make sure that your investments are returning more than what the Cost-of-Living Index takes away and set your financial goal at a realistically high figure.

TAXES AND POLITICS

As American taxpayers we are faced with two monumental problems. One is the age-old process of keeping up with the cost of living, whether the C.P.I. drops to its old level of 3.5 per cent or rises beyond the present 6.8 per cent.

The second problem is in the field of politics and taxation. During the political year of 1976 many cries were heard for tax reform. Voters and politicians alike condemned our tax structure as unfair. We can all agree that our tax structure is unfair — but what do we do about it?

One candidate said that low-income families should pay less taxes and the rich more. He also hinted that he would do away with tax loopholes — possibly including home interest deductions and capital gains benefits.

Regardless of what happens to the federal tax picture, you can bet that your local property taxes will continue to take bigger and bigger bites. In many cases you will find your property taxes escalating at higher rates than the C.P.I.

So on the federal, state and local levels we taxpayers are being squeezed. But that is only half the story! We are being robbed in a way that is so slow and painless, most people don't even realize it.

For example, consider the worker (or investor) needing a $15,000 to $86,000 income increase over the next 30 years to keep up with the cost of living. The irony is that the increase CANNOT really keep you up with the cost of living unless changes are forced upon our government.

The $86,000 cannot keep up with costs because Uncle Sam will take $36,820 or 58 per cent of a married taxpayer's income vs. only $3,010 or 25 per cent from the lower $15,000 figure. Simply stated, the more money you make the higher percentage Uncle Sam takes. And this has been happening since 1964. It's a tax bonanza for a federal government that thus far has refused to find alternate solutions.

Since 1967 the cost of living has increased through 1975 at a rate of 61.2 per cent. The tax schedules have not changed during this time. The only thing that has changed for many people is that they have slipped almost unnoticed from the 22 per cent tax bracket to the 28 per cent bracket.

Yes, the American tax system is unfair and must be changed. And we can help to change it by writing, calling, questioning and demanding it from our state and federal representatives. We cannot afford to lose further deductions and at the same time be taxed more.

HIGHER INTEREST = MORE MONEY

We, the American taxpayers, are caught between an often rising CPI on one hand and a graduated tax structure on the other. With each advancing year we must earn more just to keep up with expenses.

I can't give you any simple solutions to the problem, but I can pass along some ideas which might help make the future a little bit better. For starters, always attempt to get the highest interest rates possible. If your portfolio can average a 12 rather than 10 per cent return, you will be many dollars ahead. As much as $125,000—due to the magic of "compounding figures."

Continuing with the 30-year example, a person shooting for an income of $86,000 with his funds invested at 10 per cent, would need a lump sum of $860,000 working for him. However, an investor earning 12 per cent would need less capital—only $716,640.

In addition, the investor who is earning 12 per cent will be making a lot more money and at a much faster rate. You will see what I mean with the following example. It is based upon the theoretical assumption that an investor begins with $10,000 and then reinvests all of his principal and interest for 30 years.

Beginning Capital	Interest Rate Earned	Total
10,000	10%	$174,494
10,000	12%	299,599
10,000	15%	662,117

Of course, we have taxes and expenses to pay. But this example does demonstrate how money can multiply and what can happen when an investor has a well defined goal and sticks with it. It also demonstrates what a big difference can be made with what seems like relatively insignificant increases in interest rates. Prove it to yourself! For 10 per cent interest multiply $10,000 thirty times by 1.10. For an 11 per cent return multiply by 1.11 and so on.

On the surface, one can easily see that second investing can be rewarding. Now let's get into the meat of the subject.

II

Deeds of Trust
and Mortgages

Investing in what are often called "junior liens" can truly be a successful and rewarding experience. A portfolio of these loans can help to insure a secure retirement or a happy future.

Second investing isn't really difficult and doesn't take a lot of your time. But like any worthwhile investment vehicle, you must take time to learn the basics. And because most people reading this book are novices, the next three chapters are designed to give you the basic facts you will need to make your program work. You must learn to stand before you walk — and you must walk before you run.

THE NUTS AND BOLTS OF A LOAN

It is rare when a person buys real estate for cash. The accepted procedure is to "take out" a loan on the property.

This loan or debt is evidenced in writing by what is called a "promissory note." To give the lender added assurance that the note will be paid when due, it is customary to provide some specific security for the obligation. The trust deed or mortgage is the instrument used for the security device.

The important thing to remember here is that your loan will always consist of two documents — the note and the mortgage or trust deed. The note is the borrower's promise to pay but the mortgage and trust deed make his property the collateral for the loan. It's quite simple — a default on the loan (promissory note) means that the borrower will lose his property.

A promissory note, incidentally, is a negotiable instrument which is freely transferable. However, for it to be fully transferable

it must contain seven elements. There is nothing tricky here as it would be sheer foolishness if any were left out. They are:
1. an unconditional promise,
2. in writing,
3. made by one person to another,
4. signed by the maker,
5. engaging to pay on demand or at a fixed or determinable future time,
6. a sum of money,
7. to order or to bearer.

SECOND POSITION

A loan secured by real property can be in a first, second, third or fourth position. The only appreciable difference between a first and junior loan is the position of recordation. In other words, the "first" is the senior loan and it is in first position in the event of a foreclosure. A second then would be in second position, etc.

Foreclosure of a second in no way disrupts the position of the holder of the first. On the other side of the coin, if the first holder forecloses, he wipes out the claim of the second holder because the second is subordinate to the claims of the first.

In order to protect his interest, the second mortgage holder must "bring current" the first in order to protect his interests. Because of this I do not recommend putting all of your money into second investments. It is always wise to hold out a small portion of your funds in case you ever need to make up back payments on a first loan.

While this may seem rather complicated now, bear with me. As we go on you will see that foreclosure is not an overburdening problem. In fact for some investors it has been an unexpected bonanza.

COMPARING TRUST DEEDS AND MORTGAGES

Until this point I have considered deeds of trust and mortgages to be one and the same. But this is definitely not the case.

While both are legal instruments which when signed, acknowledged and recorded make a parcel of real estate security for full payment of the accompanying loan, there are many important differences.

Most of the differences have to do with standardization and foreclosure.

The deed of trust, also accurately called the trust deed, is very standardized. You will find little difference in this document from state to state. It is clean and simple.

The mortgage, on the other hand, often varies greatly from state to state. And most of these differences are in the area of foreclosure, so important to the investor's security.

Let's take a closer look at six areas where these differences are most pronounced.

1. *Parties:*
   In a mortgage there are two parties, a mortgagor (borrower) and a mortgagee (lender). The mortgagor gives the mortgagee a lien upon his property as security for the loan. A lien can be thought of as a legal hold or debt against a property.

   In a deed of trust there are three parties: the trustor (borrower), the trustee and the beneficiary (lender). The borrower conveys the title to his property to the trustee as security for the obligation owed to the lender. The title is "reconveyed" to the borrower when he pays off the debt owed to the lender.

   In the event the borrower fails to perform as per the agreement, the property is sold at public sale by the trustee for the satisfaction of the debt. In regards to deeds of trust, it is often a title company that acts as trustee.

2. *Title:*
   A mortgage does not usually convey title, it creates a lien. In a deed of trust the title is conveyed to a trustee, although for practical purposes it is a lien also. In both cases, possession of the property remains with the borrower.

3. *Statute of Limitations:*
   With a mortgage, an action to foreclose is barred when the statute of limitations runs out on the principal obligation (the note). In a deed of trust the rights of the lender against the property are not ended when the statute has run out on the note, because the trustee has title and can still sell to pay off the debt.

4. *Remedy:*
   With a mortgage, the only remedy the lender has is foreclosure, unless the mortgage contains a power of sale, in which event such power may be exercised. In a deed of trust, alternate remedies of trustee's sale or foreclosure are permitted.

5. *Redemption:*
   Under a mortgage that has been foreclosed by court action, the borrower has a right to redeem for anywhere from six and 18

months. But with a deed of trust (or mortgage with power of sale) the debtor has a limited right of reinstatement of the loan after default is filed, but no right of redemption. The sale is absolute.

6. *Satisfaction:*

Upon full payment of a mortgage, the lender must execute and deliver to the borrower a certificate that the mortgage has been paid off. The certificate should then be recorded.

Under a deed of trust, the borrower or his assignee, after final payment, should procure the note, deed of trust and a request for full reconveyance from the lender. These documents are then given to the trustee and recorded.

FIRST CHOICE TO THE DEED OF TRUST

Whenever there is a choice, most investors prefer to use the deed of trust because of its greater security features and ease of foreclosure. Security is lessened when a mortgagee has to get a court date to foreclose and then wait maybe 12 months before he can sell the property.

Now that we have established important and basic differences between trust deeds and mortgages, I'll refer to them by their proper names. Whenever I am writing about common properties of mortgages and deeds of trust, I will use the term "second" or "junior lien."

At the present time the United States is fairly evenly divided between usage of mortgage and deeds of trust. And a few states will accept either instrument. The chart on page 50 indicates which states use the deed of trust or the mortgage.

The chart was basically compiled from the "Martindale-Hubbell Law Directory," Volume VI, Law Digests, Uniform Acts, ABA Section, 1976 edition. If you have any question about the real property laws or legal interest rates in your state, I recommend this book for easy reference. It should be found in most large libraries.

As you have probably guessed, second financing is a valuable tool and is usually much more popular in those states that use the deed of trust. States like Arizona that have recently legalized trust deeds as well as mortgages have found that in a relatively short period of time the trust deed has all but replaced the mortgage.

If you bought this book — and happen to live in a "mortgage" state like Kansas or Ohio — don't get frustrated and give up just yet. All is not lost as you have two good choices.

First of all you can proceed with second investments using the mortgage and still make money. You will probably find that in your state there is a greater need for second money than in deed of trust states because the secondary market demands aren't being satisfied.

Your second choice would be to "ship" your money to a high interest state like Nevada that uses the deed of trust. I'll tell you more about how to do this later in the book.

BAD NEWS SPREADS

From the start of my real estate career in 1965, I have talked with hundreds of people who wanted no part of second investments. Many would rather let their money rot in a low interest savings account than to carry a second.

The main reason for this distrust of seconds turned out to be quite simple. The average person does not even know that there is a difference between mortgages and deeds of trust. They remembered that Uncle Joe lost some money with a second mortgage back in the Depression. But what is amazing is that most of the people I talked with live in California—a state that has been exclusively using the trust deed for a long time.

Bad news spreads—but don't be misled by it or you will be the loser. The point to remember is that deeds of trust are very safe and secure. While a small number of investors have lost money with mortgages, I HAVE NEVER MET ANYONE WHO HAS BEEN "WIPED OUT" with a second deed of trust investment.

III

Terms, Conditions and Clauses

Several years ago I had a very unusual salesman working for me. He certainly was successful, but when he did something he always seemed to do it backwards.

One day this salesman came bouncing into the office and announced that he had just taken a new listing. He then reached into his inside coat pocket and produced his luncheon napkin. On one side of the napkin was an agreement he had obtained. It was a signed and dated statement which authorized Wells Realty to obtain a buyer in consideration for a 6 per cent commission.

It truly was a listing agreement — a short form one at that. Even though the contract was not handsomely prepared on our standard listing agreement, it was legal and the property later sold.

I am not recommending that you take convenient short cuts like my salesman did. But his story does illustrate the importance of the terms and clauses that make up your second. You could have the most completely printed form found anywhere, but if you leave out just one vital clause it might not be worth the paper it's printed on.

Much of this chapter might overwhelm you with the first reading. But don't let it get you down because at the end of the chapter I am going to tell you how to get your note and security device correctly drawn so that you will have absolutely no worries. And it won't even cost you a penny.

As stated before, a mortgage or trust deed is always accompanied by a promissory note — often called an "installment note." Both your security device (mortgage or trust deed) and the note are made up of important and standard conditions plus your terms plus vital clauses or attachments which in some cases must be added to the documents. I'll start out by explaining the necessary clauses.

CLAUSES NOT TO FORGET

There are two "clauses" which you will always want to be part of your agreement. And there is one which you will never want—the subordination clause.

1. *Acceleration Clause:* This is a standard statement which should always be part of both your security device and promissory note. This clause allows the investor to demand full payment on his note if the borrower sells, alienates the title to his property in any way or fails to pay any installments of principal, interest, taxes or insurance when due.

   The acceleration clause enhances both the security of your note and its desirability to another lender in the event you ever sell it. It also protects the investor from being put into the hands of an unqualified borrower if the property is sold.

   There are two common types of acceleration clauses. The first brings due all sums of principal and interest at the option of the lender if the borrower fails to pay any installment of principal, interest, taxes, etc.

   The second type, generally called a "due on sale or alienation" clause, provides that all sums of principal and interest become due and payable upon the sale, transfer or further encumbrance of the property.

   Most notes and security devices will contain both types of acceleration clauses. It is important that you make sure they do. In California and many other states your instruments would be invalid unless the clause is printed in its entirety on all documents securing the loan obligation.

   Refer to the sample installment note on pages 98 and 99. The acceleration clauses are contained in two separate paragraphs (second and third to last).

2. *Request for Notice of Default and Sale:* As a second holder, you will want to be notified if your borrower is in default with his "first" loan. You will understand when foreclosures are discussed in the next chapter that the second holder must be in a situation to cure the default on the first (bring back payments current) in order to "save" his investment. Because a borrower may be delinquent with the first loan but current with the second, all your loans must be accompanied by the "Request for Notice" document.

   This important document requires the county recorder's

office to notify you in writing if the first loan holder files for foreclosure. It is your signal to go into action!

The request for notice must contain the recording date applying to the trust deed or mortgage plus the name and address of the person wanting the notification. The recorder notes the request on the margin of the record for the trust deed or mortgage. In the event of a default, the lender must be notified within a specified time.

Although some trust deed or mortgage (with power of sale) forms may have the request for notice printed in the instrument, many do not. If the request for notice clause is not in your document, you must record a separate form, like the one shown on pages 100 and 101.

Because you cannot afford to take any chances, I urge you to always double check to make sure that any "second" you are buying or originating has the request for notice clause. Protect yourself from the very beginning.

3. *Subordination clause:* A discussion of the subordination clause does not really belong in this book because it does not apply to "seconds."

A subordination clause is an agreement providing that a loan will be subordinated in priority to any specified existing or anticipated future lien. It is mostly used by land developers. In other words, this clause automatically converts an original first into a second or the original second into a third. By allowing this to happen, you will severely affect the equity of your second as well as its future salability.

There could come a time, however, when you are approached by a borrower asking you to subordinate to a home improvement loan. This could mean dropping you from second to third position. I would handle this situation by carefuly reviewing the current loan (payment history, equity, etc.) and then if all indicators are favorable create a new loan. All expenses for this plus a prepayment penalty on the original second would be borne by the borrower.

TERMS OF THE SECOND

By "terms" I mean those important features of your second that are negotiated between you and the borrower prior to final settlement. The better "terms" you have the more money you will make. They include interest rates; duration or length of the loan;

method and amount of payment; prepayment penalty; and late charges. Let's take a closer look.

1. *Interest rates:* Almost every state in the union has a maximum legal interest rate with a written contract and a lower legal rate of interest without a written contract. For our purposes we are interested only in the maximum rate with contract. And I mean maximum — if your state allows a 10 per cent top interest rate then never be a nice guy and settle for 9 per cent. If for any unforeseen reason you decide to sell your loan at a later date you will suffer by paying a greater discount.

   Your main criteria for selecting an interest rate should be based upon your state's maximum contract rate. See the chart on page 52. There is also a possibility that in your area — because of supply or demand — the market will just not bring the maximum rate, especially when the top legal rate exceeds 18 per cent. If you are not able to get at least 10 per cent — then I recommend that you seriously consider sending your money to another state. In Chapter VI, I explain methods of selecting a competent loan broker.

   It is against the law — or what is called usurious — if you receive more than the legal interest rate. And believe me, most states have a penalty for lenders that exceed the usury limit. Typical examples would be a forfeiture of 2½ times the interest charges in California to simply the excess rate applied to the principal in Missouri.

   As a private lender you cannot charge the borrower with any fees that would increase his interest rate beyond that allowed by law. By doing so the loan would be considered usurious. A loan broker, however, may receive a commission from the borrower's funds without violating usury laws. That is because he is not lending his own money but the funds of a third party.

   In most states the addition of a prepayment penalty or late charge does not jeopardize the usury limit.

2. *Duration of the loan:* There is no set rule on how many years your second should run. Most of them are for a three- to five-year duration. But many larger commercial seconds go as many as 20 years. Although it largely depends upon your personal preference, I wouldn't recommend going over five years with a second secured by residential property.

3. *Method and Amount of Payment:* There are two important questions to ask yourself when determining the amount and method of payment. First, how fast do you want your money returned? Secondly, what is the ability of the borrower to make the monthly payments selected?

If you want your money returned as fast as possible you would need a fully amortized loan. This means a loan that is paid in equal monthly installments so that with the last payment the remaining principal and interest are paid in full. The opposite extreme would be an interest-only loan in which the entire principal balance would remain at the end of the loan. There is a lot to be said about both approaches — so keep an open mind for now and I'll tackle this problem in detail later on.

Your third and most popular approach to pay-back would be a compromise between full amortization and interest only. For instance a loan that repays 1 per cent per month (on a three-year, 10 per cent note) will leave 93 per cent of the principal balance unpaid compared to a loan that repays 2 per cent per month which will leave 51 per cent unpaid.

Sometimes the method and amount of payment will be determined by the borrower's ability and situation.

If your borrower is an investor who is using maximum leverage to buy rental property (as outlined in "The Monopoly Game") he will want an interest-only loan. At the end of the term he will be in an excellent position to either sell or refinance the property.

But if your borrower is a homeowner who has consolidated debts from payments of $400 to $200 a month, he probably should have a fully amortized loan. If his payments aren't amortized or at least high enough to leave very little principal at the end of the term, he is going to be in trouble again and may be forced to sell his home.

The following remaining balance chart shows how much of the principal balance remains after a full year with a $1,000 loan at 10 per cent with a five-year due date (next page).

Note that a loan with a 1½ per cent monthly payback will have a balance of $721 after three full years. And after five years the borrower will owe a balloon payment of $484 and the investor's earnings will be $384 for the full term. While on the surface the chart shows that an investor can earn more with an interest-only loan than with a fully amortized one, this is not necessarily true as I will demonstrate.

REMAINING BALANCES
for $1000 at 10% interest

Type of Payback	Monthly Payment	Year 1	Year 2	Year 3	Year 4	Year 5	Total Interest Earned
Interest Only	$ 8.33	1,000	1,000	1,000	1,000	1,000	$500
1%	10.00	980	956	930	902	871	471
1½%	15.00	917	824	721	609	484	384
Fully Amortized	21.25	838	658	460	242	0	275

4. *Prepayment Penalty:* in most states a prepayment penalty is a legal method of enabling the investor to earn an extra 15 to 20 per cent on his investment. In North Carolina—which allows up to 12 per cent interest—prepayment penalties are not allowed. But this is the exception rather than the rule.

A prepayment penalty is also an excellent method for discouraging early payoffs. It would be unrealistic to expect an investor to set up a five-year loan and then have it repaid without penalty after just a few months.

There is one type of loan, however, for which I do not necessarily recommend a prepayment penalty. That is the "purchase money" second made by a homeowner to facilitate the sale. In this case the penalty might scare off the buyer. Yet it is wise to remember that if there are plans to sell the note, a greater discount may be suffered because of the missing prepayment penalty.

Typical prepayment penalties would be fees equal to six months interest or 4 per cent of the current principal balance. With the penalty based on the "current principal balance" the amount becomes progressively smaller on amortized loans.

Because of the declining balance of amortized loans, some investors will base the penalty on the original balance rather than the current balance. This, of course, will bring a higher return. Be sure and check on your state laws and customs before fixing your prepayment penalty rates.

The length of time a prepayment penalty remains in effect is also a matter of choice. It can range through the first six months of the loan or through the complete term. A length that is fair to both borrower and lender would be for the first three years on a five-year loan.

Two words to be very careful of when setting up the terms of your second are "or more."

"Or more" means that the borrower has the right to pay off more than the fixed monthly payment without penalty.

5. *Late Charges:* As with prepayment penalties, always add a late charge to your note when it is legal to do so. They are a great help in making the borrower responsible with his payments. Most people will soon learn that it is ridiculous to keep paying an extra $5 or $10 each month. And of course when the payment is late you pocket the penalty which adds to your profits.

Most states have laws that regulate the dollar amounts for late charges. Where it's legal, I recommend a charge between 5 and 10 per cent of the monthly payment. Thus a second with $100 per month payments would require a late charge of $5 or $10. You will want to use the higher charges with an interest-only note because the monthly payments will be much lower than with an amortized loan.

There are two basic ways to collect your penalty. One would be to take the charge out of the principal part of the borrower's payment. The second and preferred method is to notify the borrower and demand the late charge payment. The latter method will hurt the pocketbook a little more and keep the borrower on his toes next time around.

STANDARD CONDITIONS

In addition to the major contract clauses and the important and detailed terms worked out by you and the borrower, there are other printed conditions and terms of your security device with which you should be aware.

Although many such conditions can exist, I will only attempt to cover the most important here. They include: fire insurance; deficiency judgment; power of sale and right of redemption.

1. *Fire Insurance:* Obviously your loan would be in jeopardy if your secured property burned to the ground. I don't think you could ever find a printed trust deed or mortgage that didn't have a "fire insurance" clause. But to be on the safe side always check this out and make sure the terms are to your liking.

In part, the fire insurance clause from the sample deed of trust on page 102 reads: "To provide, maintain and deliver to beneficiary fire insurance satisfactory to and with loss payable to beneficiary. The amount collected under any fire or other insurance policy may be applied by beneficiary upon any indebtedness secured hereby and in such order as beneficiary may determine, or at option of beneficiary the entire amount so collected or any part thereof may be released to trustor (borrower)."

A simple translation means that the borrower is to purchase and maintain a fire insurance policy which will be delivered to the lender. By the policy being in the lender's possession, you are assured the protection is current and adequate. It also states that in case of fire you (the lender who is the beneficiary of the policy) may apply the funds for reconstruction of the property or to pay off the indebtedness (loan).

As a second loan holder, you will not receive the original fire insurance policy unless there are two separate policies. The original will go to the first lender (referred to as the "first loss payee") and a copy will go to you—the "second loss payee."

Although two separate fire policies can be written on a property in order to cover a subsequent second loan, it is more common to extend the coverage of the original policy.

Because a fire can never destroy the land (often valued at 20 per cent of the total market value of a home), you might be asked to forego fire insurance when the first loan already exceeds or equals 80 per cent of the market value. I wouldn't go along with this request for two reasons. First of all the equity based on market value may be incorrect and secondly with many homes appreciating in value at 8 to 15 per cent a year, the borrower would be foolish not to want maximum coverage. As homes increase in value so do construction costs.

2. *Deficiency Judgment:* A deficiency judgment is basically the statutory right of the lender to sue the borrower if sale under foreclosure does not bring enough money to pay off the note. With the present trend of escalating home prices the need to sue for a deficiency judgment may be rare.

While the exact laws regarding deficiency judgments will vary a little between states, it is common to find "purchase money" loans exempt. In other words a seller who takes back a "purchase money" loan to help with the sale of his property cannot get a deficiency judgment.

3. *Power of sale:* A "power of sale" is almost always part of a deed of trust and sometimes part of a mortgage. The power of sale gives the trustee (third party in a deed of trust) the right to sell a property upon default rather than go through a possible lengthy court sale proceeding. By the same token, a mortgage with power of sale thus authorizes the mortgagee (lender) to sell a property without court proceedings.

   I previously gave reasons why a deed of trust was a better security device than a mortgage. Partially this is because of lengthy redemption periods required by mortgages without power of sale. However, some states allow mortgages to contain a power of sale and thus often beat the poorly designed redemption problem. If you live in a mortgage state be sure and use the "power of sale" form if both are allowed. It can make a big difference. In Rhode Island, for instance, a borrower has a three-year right of redemption unless the document has the power of sale.

4. *Right of Redemption:* You have probably discovered that the "right of redemption" and "power of sale" have something in common. They do — but yet they are two distinctly different items. A right of redemption gives the borrower under most mortgages a period of time in which he can reclaim title to his property. Of course, the borrower must make all back and delinquent payments and penalty charges to do so.

   While not many borrowers will redeem their property, it puts the lender in a bad position because he must wait the lapse of this right before making any final disposition of the property. Because of this right, states that do not allow a "power of sale" and have lengthy redemption periods do not experience very much second mortgage activity.

   If you live in states like Delaware, Florida and Louisiana, you won't have a problem because there is no right of redemption.

   In South Dakota there is a six-month right of redemption even with a power of sale. Examples of states with a fairly typical one-year redemption period are Hawaii, Kansas and Maine.

WHEN THE BORROWER PAYS OFF

When your borrower pays off his loan or makes his final payment, another document is required. If your security form is the trust deed, this document is called the Deed of Reconveyance.

Basically this form is used in the following manner. After the beneficiary (lender) receives the last payment, he signs his name to the backside of the deed of trust (where it reads "request for full reconveyance") and then returns it to the trustor (borrower) along with the promissory note. The borrower then takes these two documents to the trustee (normally an escrow or title company). For a small charge the title company issues and records a deed of reconveyance which removes the lien from county records. Soon after recordation, this document is mailed to the borrower.

This procedure should be altered slightly when the borrower wants to pay off the note before the due date. Don't initially accept his money or sign the back of the trust deed but instead direct the borrower to the title company. The title company (or loan broker if you are using his services) will send you a form entitled "Request for Full Reconveyance" which you are required to sign along with a statement asking for the amount of principal and interest due you. Send these documents back along with the original note and deed of trust. Your money will be on its way after recordation.

The procedure is much the same when a mortgage is paid off. Only the document is called a "full release of mortgage" or a "satisfaction of mortgage." Because the mortgage does not have a third party (trustee), the lender can simply have the document notarized and then recorded in the county of the subject property.

THE EASY WAY

Unless you have already been using promissory notes, mortgages and acceleration clauses, you are probably wiping your brow now and thinking that "there are certainly easier ways of making money." But all is not lost!

There are two easy methods an investor can use to maintain his investment portfolio. One way is to use the experienced and professional help of a loan broker. Chapter VI is devoted to this "armchair" approach where you can sit back and let a pro do all of your work.

The second method is designed for the "do-it-yourself" specialist. It's so easy that you will not even have to obtain, fill out and record your instruments. Let a title company do it for you! Or if your state does not have full service title companies — see a settlement or real estate attorney. Any fees, which will be modest, should be paid for by the borrower. These services should not cost you anything.

Even though a title company is in business to sell policies of title insurance, most perform excellent escrow services. Go see them when you are ready to draw terms on your second. They are more than willing—for a small charge between $10 and $25—to type your terms on the proper documents. They will also "record" your papers if you ask for this service. And you can be sure they will attempt to sell you a policy of title insurance.

TITLE INSURANCE

Title insurance can be simply described as a policy of insurance written by a title company to protect the property owner against loss if the title is imperfect. Therefore it is an added protection for the lender too.

And most importantly, for any purposes, each policy of title insurance is preceded by a preliminary search of the records to make sure there are no other recorded deeds or liens against the property.

For instance, your borrower may tell you about his $15,000 first mortgage with the Bank of ABC but purposely forget to tell you about a $3,000 lien against his property by XYZ Finance Company and a $2,000 delinquent tax judgment. Because your borrower's two liens are recorded, your policy of title insurance will not protect you against them. If you proceed with the loan you will be in a shaky "fourth" position, as loan position is basically determined by which lien is recorded first.

But because of the preliminary search of title, you will be warned in time about problem liens. In most cases you would either refuse to make the loan or perhaps even increase the size of your loan to pay off any liens that would force you into third position.

In the above example, if the $3,000 lien by XYZ Finance Company was recorded but not "picked up" by the title company, your policy of title insurance would protect you.

Always have your borrower pay for a policy of title insurance. If your second and a new first loan are being "closed" together in the same escrow, then the title insurance fee will be only about $10.

If your second is being handled in its own special escrow, then the charge would be in the neighborhood of $70 to $120.

IV

Servicing
Your Loan

Good money management starts with a realistic budget, contains an element of discipline and ends with a set of well kept records.

I know of one man who has been investing in seconds and rental homes for several years now. He estimated his investment equities at close to $100,000. He was naturally nervous when the IRS called him in for a routine audit. My friend didn't keep very good records, though, so it took him hours upon hours to prepare for the audit.

He got through the audit with flying colors—no significant changes with his prior tax payment. But one interesting fact did emerge. He discovered his investment worth wasn't $100,000 but only $85,000. It is obvious my friend didn't keep good records.

Servicing your loans requires not only good record-keeping but you must also learn how to make collections, handle delinquent loans and file for foreclosure. All of this and more will be discussed in this chapter.

KEEP YOUR DOCUMENTS SAFE

For demonstration purposes in this chapter, I am going to assume that you have already located a qualified borrower, apraised his home (see Chapter V), and have had the title company prepare and record your documents. The initial work is done—you have your first loan.

Within a few weeks after the transaction "closes" you will receive from the county recorder your "recorded" deed of trust (or mortgage) and request for notice of default. At about the same time the title company will send you the promissory note, the policy of title insurance and the copy of original fire insurance policy. Along with these you will have other information from both the title company (lender's instructions and preliminary title search) and your own files on the buyer's history and property.

It is important to keep all of the documents. You should fasten at least one copy of the documents inside a manila envelope which would be labeled with the borrower's name followed by the address of the secured property.

The note and security device are the most important of the documents. Although the deed of trust or mortgage can be reproduced from county records, the note cannot. If it is lost or destroyed it may be impossible to replace unless your borrower is nice enough to sign a new one for you.

I suggest making a copy of these two instruments and then place the copies in your manila folder and place the originals in a bank or savings safe deposit box.

COLLECTING PAYMENTS

About one month after your loan is recorded you will receive your first payment. There is a one-month lapse, because interest always goes backwards. In other words, the loan records on June 1 but the first payment is not due until July 1. This first payment is principal plus interest for the month of June.

Your collections will be made a lot easier if you thoroughly explain two items to your borrower. First, make sure he knows exactly where to send the payment and exactly how to make out the check "payee" line.

Secondly, tell him that you will strictly enforce the "late charge" penalty if you do not receive his payment within the grace period. Explain that you will not make a trip to his home to collect payments nor will you tolerate "bounced" checks.

I will sometimes make an exception with the late charge penalty in order to gain the borrower's good will and full support. If his payment history is good, I will stretch the penalty period a few days if I am told in advance that a payment will be late. I would much rather know what is happening than be kept in the dark.

Without a doubt, the best way to keep full control of your loans is to either make the collections yourself or have your loan broker do it. But there is one other good alternative. Your bank or savings and loan association will probably be more than happy to collect the payments for a minimal monthly fee (usually 50¢ to $2).

Not only will your funds earn interest, but the bank or savings and loan will help keep limited records of your accounts. Some savings and loans will even send a borrower a letter when he is late with his payments. But for the most part, banks and savings and loans will not manage your loans. All decisions and enforcement of late penalties will still be up to you.

An important thing to remember is that not all banks or savings and loans are the same. You may want to shop around for the best "deal" if you don't like the terms offered by your own lending institution.

RECORD-KEEPING MADE SIMPLE

Collecting loan payments is one thing—but keeping detailed and accurate records is something else again. For many people keeping track of their money is quite simple. But you might be surprised at the number of investors that I have known that are almost totally baffled by simple bookkeeping.

If your investment portfolio is handled by a loan broker, then you will not have to worry about bookkeeping. But if you are handling your own portfolio you will need to keep detailed and accurate records. Not only will you want to know how you stand at a moment's notice but Uncle Sam is very interested in your records, too.

The best advice I can give is to maintain a simple yearly ledger record of all payments that you receive. Keep this form in a safe and easily accessible place so that you can record all payments the day you receive them. Get into a habit of not cashing any of the checks until you record and compute the payment and mail a receipt to the borrower.

The borrower's receipt, incidentally, can simply be a loan payment booklet often furnished free of charge by a bank or title company. The borrower should send this booklet along with each payment. You then record the date of payment; interest paid; amounts credited on interest and principal; and balance of unpaid principal. After this is done send the loan payment booklet back to the borrower—it then becomes his receipt of payment.

The loan payment booklet—and the bother of monthly mailings—can be eliminated if you choose instead to furnish your borrower with an amortization schedule. This schedule should show all monthly breakdowns of principal and interest. They are inex-

INVESTMENT PROFILE - 1976 AT A GLANCE

Borrower's Name Property Address	Pymt. Terms	Due Date	Mnthly. Pymt. Due	Late Chgs. Coll.	Beg. Balance	Jan.	Feb.	March	April	May	June	July	Aug.	Sept.	Oct.	Nov.	Dec.	Year End Balance	I/P
Gordon Hay 142 Smith Rd.	Int. Only	7-1-77	1st	-0-		25.-	25.-	25	25	25	25	25	25	25	25	25.-	25	—	I
					3,000													3,000.	P
George Losey 1631 Broadway Pl.	Full	12-1-76	1st	-0-		7.05	6.49	5.92	5.35	4.78	4.20	3.61	3.02	2.43	1.83	1.22	0.01		I
					845.86	67.32	67.88	68.44	69.01	69.59	70.17	70.75	71.34	71.94	72.54	73.14	73.75	-0-	P
Bob Easthouse 41 Valley Ct.	Full	12-1-78	1st	20.00		21.95	21.42	20.89	20.36	19.82	19.28	18.73	18.18	17.62	17.06	16.49	15.92		I
					2,633.89	63.04	63.56	64.09	64.63	65.17	65.71	66.26	66.81	67.37	67.93	68.49	69.06	1,841.77	P
Kay Thornton 210 Jennifer	1%	12-1-80	15th	-0-		40.79	40.72	40.64	40.56	40.43	40.40	40.32	40.24	40.16	40.03	40.00	39.91		I
					4,895.29	9.21	9.23	9.36	9.44	9.52	9.60	9.68	9.76	9.84	9.92	10.00	10.09	4,779.61	P
Joe Janis 1141 Arthur Road	1½%	7-1-80	10th	30.00		40.25	39.96	39.67	39.33	39.02	38.78	38.43	38.13	37.27	37.56	37.25	36.93		I
					4,836.59	34.75	35.04	35.33	35.62	35.92	36.22	36.52	36.32	37.13	37.44	37.75	38.07	4,393.93	P
Dauna Baldini 66 Oak Knoll Rd.	Int. Only	6-30-79	15th	10.00		66.67	66.67	66.67	66.67	66.67	66.67	66.67	66.67	66.67	66.67	66.67	66.67		I
					8,000													8,000.	P
Diana Weber 31 Burns Court	Full	6-1-81	1st	-0-						(New)	33.33	31.90	32.47	32.03	31.59	31.14	30.70		I
										$4,000	51.65	52.09	52.52	52.96	53.40	53.84	54.29	3,602.25	P
Interest Totals				60.00	22,205.59	201.71	200.82	198.71	197.27	195.78	217.66	215.66	223.71	221.28	219.74	217.72	215.74	2,545.37	I
Principal Totals						174.32	175.71	177.22	178.72	180.26	233.35	235.30	236.75	238.24	241.23	243.22	245.26	25,644.56	P

by Glubetich Enterprises, 1977

pensive and can be purchased from any number of computer or financial service firms.

The ledger form I recommend is shown at the left. The form was developed for some of my investors who were habitually losing track of a payment or two each year. The form allows you to keep all the information you need on one simple sheet. It has 12 monthly columns which are divided so that you can compute the interest and principal portion of each payment and then total them at the bottom. This way you always know where your accounts stand with just a glance.

The interest totals ($2,545.37) on the sample are computed by adding the interest columns to the left of the total. The year-end principal balance is derived by adding the "P" columns directly above the "total" box.

The column marked "late charges" should be done in pencil so that you can keep a running total of late charges received. As you can see on the sample, I also circle the monthly totals to indicate that a borrower was late and thus charged a penalty. In this way you can easily spot your most troublesome accounts.

These "at a glance" ledger forms are available in pads of 24 for $2.95 from Dave Glubetich, 12 Gregory Lane, Pleasant Hill, California 94523.

COMPUTING MONTHLY INTEREST

To keep accurate records you must learn how to break down each payment into interest and principal portions. You will want this information for your "at a glance" ledger as well as for your borrower's receipt.

The reasons are obvious. If the borrower wants to pay off the loan you must be able to tell him how much money he will need to do so. And when tax time comes you will need to know how much interest was earned during the year. And if you don't keep up with your bookkeeping on a monthly basis you will have a horrendous job at the end of the year.

There are no computations necessary for an interest-only loan because the principal balance remains the same. On all other loans you must compute the interest and principal unless you have a printed "amortization schedule."

It is not really a difficult task to compute monthly interest charges. It is a four-step mathematical process that involves only simple division and subtraction. The four-step formula requires that you have the following advance information: interest rate; loan payment amount; and previous balance of unpaid principal. The following example (and formula) is based upon a 10 per cent interest loan. If you are computing 9 or 12 per cent interest you must multiply by .09 or .12 rather than move the decimal point.

A SIMPLE FORMULA

1. Determine 10% of last balance of unpaid principle by multiplying by .10 or moving the decimal point one place to the left.
2. Divide by 12 (representing 12 months). This gives you the amount of interest paid.
3. Subtract the interest paid from the monthly payment. This gives you the amount of principal paid.
4. Subtract the amount of principal paid from the last unpaid principal balance. This gives you the current balance of the unpaid principal.

THE FORMULA AT WORK

(The example is a 10% note that repays at $30 per month. The last balance of unpaid principal was $2,504.15.)

Amount Paid	Credited on Interest	Credited on Principal	Balance of unpaid principal
			$2,504.15*
$30.00	$20.87	$9.13	$2,495.02
30.00	20.79	9.21	2,485.81
30.00	20.72	9.28	2,476.66

*(Computations are started by reducing $2,504.15 to 250.415 by moving the decimal point one place to the left. Then divide by 12 to get 20.866 which is rounded off to $20.87.)

Note how the interest decreases and the principal increases with each ensuing loan payment.

With newer loans more is paid on interest than principal. For instance, a five-year, $5,000 note at 10 per cent interest pays $463.48 on interest the first year and only $66.45 the fifth and final year.

HOW TO HANDLE DELINQUENCIES

Delinquencies usually fall into one of two categories — serious and not serious.

The so-called "not serious" delinquencies can be a real pain in the neck but they are not indicative of a forthcoming default. They usually result from a borrower forgetting to mail in his payment or a temporary problem like vacation or money shortage. A money shortage can come from paying off a large medical bill rather than your "second" or perhaps a temporary layoff or job change. In most cases the borrower will tell you the reason and make a double payment including a late charge the following month.

Theoretically, if a payment is not made on the day it is due, it can be considered delinquent. But for practical purposes it is not usually considered delinquent until 10 or 15 days later — the day upon which the late charge becomes due.

There are two practical ways of handling these minor delinquencies. The first method is to make sure your note carries a reasonably stiff late charge. And when the borrower's payment is late, enforce the penalty.

If the payment comes in a day or two late and does not include the penalty, then call or write the borrower and ask that he send you the fee now or at least include it with the next payment. If you ask for the penalty with the next payment — and you don't get it — then it is within your rights to return the payment and demand a check for the proper amount (regular payment plus late charge).

However, I caution you on one point. If you feel as I do — that life is too short to get involved in petty, escalating battles — then show a little leniency where justified.

While I would not let a habitually late payer off the hook, I might overlook a good account that is late for the first time in a dozen or so months. I might also let a borrower off the hook that calls me in advance to say why his payment will be late and to tell me when it will be made. If his payment and word are good — and if he doesn't have a history of "sob stories" — then I may excuse his late charge.

A bounced check is usually a different matter. If a payment becomes delinquent because of a bounced check I will almost always assess that late charge.

In addition to the late charge, there is one other method of controlling late payments. And that is to write a strong but polite letter to the borrower reminding him of his obligations and asking for his support and payment. If you fail with both the letter and late charge, then you may have a "serious" delinquency.

A "serious" delinquency can be described as one in which the borrower is two or more payments in arrears and the situation appears hopeless. Often because of a divorce, poor health or loss of job a borrower may be in real trouble. He may be letting the payments go on the first as well as the second loan.

Whether or not you receive notice from the county based upon your "Request for Notice of Default and Sale," you should face the seriousness of the problem and immediately file a notice of default. Don't feel sorry for the borrower and delay filing because he will still have almost four months to bring back payments current.

FILING THE NOTICE OF DEFAULT

A "notice of default" is the usual legal method of beginning the foreclosure process when a borrower is delinquent. Most importantly, this method does not involve the court process.

A notice of default can be filed by the trustee or beneficiary in a deed of trust or by the mortgagee in a mortgage that contains a "power of sale." Although it is possible for the investor or his loan broker to personally file the default notice, the accepted procedure is to file the notice through the title company that was trustee for the loan transaction.

There is a small charge for this service but it is the borrower's responsibility as he must pay all charges to cure the default.

In California and most other states, recordation of the notice of default begins a three-month waiting period before the next step begins — the publishing of a notice of sale. During this three-month period the borrower has the right to stop the default proceedings by paying all delinquencies, late fees and foreclosure charges. The investor should not accept any payments that are not the *FULL* amount. If a partial payment is accepted this may require filing a second notice of default with a second three-month waiting period.

As an investor, your real problem isn't how to file for foreclosure but when to file. As I stated before, you can and probably should file after a borrower is fully two payments in arrears. There are two exceptions. One would be when your subject home is for sale and you have been reasonably assured that escrow will be closing in the next few weeks. The second exception would be when you are in communication with the borrower and he has proven to you that the money (from sale of goods or a loan from relatives) will be forthcoming within a few days. However, beware of one thing. If your borrower is expecting money from a court settlement (inheritance, law suit judgment, etc.) you might double or triple his estimate of time. I have found the courts work in slow and mysterious ways.

FORECLOSURE BY COURT ACTION

When filing for foreclosure under most mortgages without power of sale, you must use the courts.

This procedure, if uncontested, should take between 90 and 120 days. If the borrower contests your foreclosure action, you can expect to add another month to the proceedings. An extra crowded court schedule can also add time.

Following a court decree of foreclosure, the sheriff (or court commissioner) sells the property to the highest bidder. The purchaser then gets a "certificate of sale" which is evidence that he has acquired legal title to the property, subject to certain redemption rights.

As discussed in Chapter III, the right of redemption varies from state to state. After the redemption period has passed, the purchaser is entitled to a deed from the sheriff or commissioner.

In most states, the borrower under a mortgage with redemption rights may remain in possession for the redemption period. The purchaser, however, is entitled to the rent and profits during this period unless the mortgagor later redeems, in which case they are credited to the redemption money to be paid.

COMPLETING THE FORECLOSURE

Three months after filing the notice of default, the trustee's sale period automatically begins. At this point the investor can take a harder stand because he can instruct the title company to accept only *full* payment of his note plus interest and foreclosure charges. Before the borrower only needed to bring all payments current plus interest and foreclosure charges.

At this point, the investor can also instruct the title company (or trustee) to begin the advertising period of the notice of sale. This is usually a 21-day period, after which the subject property is sold.

The notice of sale must include the street address of the

property and the time and place of sale. It must be posted on the property or in a public place and it must be advertised at least once a week during a 21-day period in a newspaper of general circulation either printed or distributed in the city or area of the subject property.

Any time after the advertising period is completed, the trustee's sale may be held. The property is sold to the highest bidder — in a manner similar to an auction. Unless there is a great deal of equity in the property, the investor will probably be the only bidder at the sale. And the investor need not be present either, because the title company can prepare a bid form, which when signed, allows the title company to make it as the opening bid. Usually this bid amount will be only for the amount of the back payments and other delinquency charges.

After making the sale, the title company will execute a "Trustee's Deed" to the purchaser. The sale thus becomes final and there is no right of redemption with foreclosures done in this manner.

HOW COMMON ARE FORECLOSURES?

Much of what I have written so far deals with foreclosure. At this point you might be wondering just what kind of an investment are seconds if you always have to be so concerned with defaults, foreclosures and redemption periods.

Put your mind at ease! "Mortgage foreclosure rates during the first quarter (1976) were the lowest they've been in five years."

The national delinquency survey of the Mortgage Bankers Association of America reports that "the proportion of mortgage loans (including deeds of trust) on which foreclosure action was started during the first quarter was 0.18 per cent, seasonally adjusted."

"The rate is down from 0.19 per cent at the end of the fourth quarter of 1975, and is the lowest it has been since mid-1971."

"Strong increases in employment and income were largely responsible for the continued decline in foreclosure rates," according to MBA chief economist John Wetmore.

You must understand defaults and always be prepared to foreclose. But as you can see, the odds of this happening are extremely low.

CAN YOU PROFIT FROM FORECLOSURE??

I am sure that most of my readers have enjoyed—as I often have—a suspenseful melodrama in which the audience rises as one to hiss the villainous banker who is about to make a huge profit by foreclosing on a poor and helpless widow. Alas! The villain never wins! But many people get the idea that in real life the villain does win a lot.

As a moneylender some people might now classify you as the villain. So the logical question is—are you going to make out like a bandit on foreclosure? The answer is *probably not*.

One hundred years ago you would have had a better chance of making a killing than now. The laws today—for both mortgages and deeds of trust—are designed to give protection to both the lender and to the borrower. There are no fast and inhumane ways of taking away someone's property. The borrower has ample time to come up with the funds necessary to cure a default. A high percentage of borrowers will go to a third party and thus place a "third" junior lien on the property. Often this "third" loan will be an amount sufficient to pay off your second. In that case it goes to the second position by paying off your loan.

If the borrower has insufficient equity (for instance loans totaling $30,000 with a home value of only $35,000) he will probably not be able to borrow more money and thus will be more vulnerable to foreclosure. But in this case the borrower isn't losing a great deal and you will not gain a great amount either.

In the above case you might not even want the home. You must realize that the back payments and delinquencies added to the $30,000 loan will probably bring the total liens to about $32,000. That leaves a true equity of only $3,000 and if you had to turn around and pay a brokerage fee to sell the home another $2,100 to $2,500 would be needed.

If you decide that you don't want a home because of poor equity position, I suggest that you tip off a Realtor or property investor about the trustee's sale. Your second plus delinquencies will probably be an easy enough cash outlay to handle. The Realtor or investor will usually be allowed to take over the first loan with a trustee's deed without any change in interest, prepayment or high loan origination fee. Policy varies with each lender so check with them.

Taking title in this manner sure beats qualifying for a new conventional loan with high closing costs. And with single family homes in 1976 appreciating at 16 per cent in many parts of the country, this $35,000 home with a small equity just might turn out to be a fine investment for someone.

I've discussed the most common foreclosure situation — the home with a relatively small amount of real equity. But occasionally you will run into a situation where the loans total only $20,000 and the value is close to $35,000. This situation, of course, opens up another solution to foreclosure. If the borrower's money problems are short term, you could rewrite your second at a larger amount. Most of the difference between your first and second junior lien would go to curing the back payments and foreclosure charges.

If for some reason you cannot or will not rewrite your loan, this large equity situation will probably create a much different atmosphere at the trustee's sale. You will undoubtedly now find a group of bidders at the sale looking for a quick profit.

A probable bidding war could cost you $4,000 to $5,000 more if you intend to be the successful bidder. The real villain has made his appearance — not the professional or amateur moneylender but the "sharks" who make a living by closely following the newspapers to find where there is human misery that they can pounce on for a quick profit with no personal risk or effort.

A METHOD OF AVOIDING FORECLOSURE

Often both the lender and the borrower will be ahead of the game if the property can be transferred without going through formal foreclosure.

I don't know of any law which prohibits the investor from purchasing the property before foreclosure. This technique is best used in a hopeless situation where the borrower has little equity and absolutely no chance of saving his home.

By having the homeowner sign a deed to the property you can save a lot of time and additional expense. To accomplish this you may have to pay the borrower a few hundred dollars for his agreement to sign over his home and move out a month or two earlier.

Cheating the foreclosure process in this manner should only be done when it will benefit both borrower and investor. If there are any potential problems, such as a first loan holder that could call his note due and payable if the sale was made without formal foreclosure, then consult an attorney for legal advice.

V

The Do-It-Yourself Approach

"Take the high road or the low road." You have the choice! One of the nicest things about secondary financing is that there are two different but equally effective methods available to create and multiply your investment portfolio.

In the next chapter I will discuss the loan broker — the competent professional who will enable you to make money with almost no risk and with very little effort.

The second approach, of course, is the do-it-yourself method. This road will also bring profit, but a little frustration at times along with a lot of self-satisfaction.

This chapter will go into all the pros and cons of the do-it-yourself method. I will show you where you can find literally hundreds of clients that are "solid gold" but they are borrowers that the loan broker won't touch. We'll go into appraising methods that you must understand to protect the security of your note.

When you are finished with this and the preceding four chapters you will be ready to embark on your own lending program. You will have gained almost as much knowledge in a few hours as I did in 11 years. All that you will lack is the field experience that helps to round out your education.

PURCHASE MONEY LOANS

Real estate law recognizes two basic types of secondary loans — "purchase money" and "hard money." Both types are very important for our purposes.

Basically a purchase money loan is one that is created and carried back by a property seller. It is a well accepted means of helping both the buyer and seller bring about a sale that might not otherwise be made. For instance, if a buyer has $7,000 to assume a low interest loan of $25,000 with a $35,000 sales price, he is obviously $3,000 short. It makes a lot of sense to assume (pay cash to the loan) a 7 per cent loan rather than refinance at perhaps 9 per cent. Not only will the monthly payments on the first be about $34 less because of the lower interest rate but the buyer can save another $1,000-plus in closing costs. And the cost to the buyer is fairly nominal — $3,000 borrowed at 10 per cent and due in five years will repay fully amortized at only $63.75 monthly.

Purchase money loans can often lead the amateur lender into trouble. Many of these owner transactions overlook late charges, prepayment penalties, request for notice of default and maximum interest rates. Often when the holder of a purchase money note decides six months later to cash in he finds to his surprise that he must pay a 20 to 30 per cent discount.

Partially because of this history, purchase money seconds enter the "resale" market with one strike against them. Part of the problem can be eliminated so that the purchase money second can bring a more normal discount of only 10 to 20 per cent. And that is by strengthening your note to make sure that it contains all the features that have been discussed so far.

The second inherent problem with purchase money seconds lies in the realm of the law and property equity.

In the event of a foreclosure, the law does not allow the lender to obtain a "deficiency judgment." That means if the sale under foreclosure does not bring enough to pay off the note, the borrower (mortgagor or trustor) cannot be sued for the balance. This does not hold true with hard money loans.

One major reason for outlawing deficiency judgments with purchase money loans is that the sale is often consummated without a formal appraisal and the buyer's equity is sometimes paper thin. Whereas most "hard money" loans originated by the mortgage broker require the borrower to have at least 20 per cent equity in the property, purchase money seconds often find the buyer getting by with as little as 10 per cent equity.

Although thin equities can cause a note to be discounted at a greater rate than one with a larger equity, I am not saying that this is always bad. I'll give you my reasons shortly.

THE PURCHASE MONEY BONANZA

As I just mentioned, the law treats purchase money differently than hard money loans. While this deprives the holder of a purchase money note (whether original maker or not) the right to obtain a deficiency judgment, there is a possible advantage in favor of the purchase money loan.

Imagine the opportunities that would open up if your purchase money loan was not limited by restrictive usury laws? If it could carry 12 or 14 per cent interest?

Apparently this is the case in California! According to renowned real estate attorney Harry B. Miller, usury laws apply to loans only. And California law treats purchase money transactions as a selling tool rather than a loan. Thus purchase money loans are exempt from usury laws in California and probably many other states. This theory has already been backed up by court decisions, according to Miller.

Further reference on the subject can be found in the new second edition of "Current Law of California Real Estate, Volume 4," by Harry D. Miller and Marvin B. Starr.

If you are not a California resident I certainly don't advise you to jump head first into a purchase money loan without first checking with legal counsel.

Once you are assured that usury or consumer code guidelines in your state have no regulatory effect over purchase money loans, you can open up new doors. However, don't be surprised if market conditions prevent you from obtaining much over the common and accepted interest rates. While you might want a 12 per cent return, you may find it tough to find a buyer willing to pay more than 10 per cent. And you will probably find that most title companies will shy away from this type of loan.

As a loan investor, you may not find any opportunities to create a purchase money loan, as they are reserved for property sellers. However, you may find it worthwhile to contact local Realtors and let them know you would be interested in buying any such loans that they may know of—for a small discount, of course. But be sure that any such loans have matured at least six months so that you leave no questions regarding possible usury law violations. If a loan is purchased directly out of escrow it may be conceived that the borrower could have raised the money to buy the loan. If the borrower is not told of this note sale, it could then be called usurious.

HARD MONEY LOANS

The term "hard money" is used to describe all secondary financing that is not considered to be "purchase money." I suspect that the term was coined because of the high costs charged to borrowers for these loans. For many, a second loan is the expensive and thus hard way to get needed money.

For our purposes, I am going to consider two types of hard money loans. The first type, which is discussed in this chapter, is the loan made directly by the do-it-yourself lender to the borrower.

The second type of hard money loan is the loan made by you—via your loan broker—to the borrower. It can be considered a three-party loan and it is by far the most expensive of the two types for the borrower. Chapter VI will deal exclusively with this type of hard money loan.

KNOW YOUR STATE LAWS

While I have attempted to give you a clear picture of the basic knowledge you will need to become a successful and prosperous money lender, there is one important area that I cannot cover in this book. To do so would require a volume of 1,000 or more pages. This missing link is a basic understanding of specific laws and customs in your state (or where you are planning to invest) that affect the secondary loan market.

There are seven major areas of concern. And each state is apt to have different laws or regulations governing them. If you are going to invest your money—particularly on your own—then be prepared so you won't get into trouble.

It is not difficult to "get in touch" with your laws. Write or call your state real estate commissioner or the state department of finance and/or banking. In some cases you may need to get information from more than one department. It's not difficult to do as I have found them to be most cooperative.

These seven areas of concern—areas where the laws will vary the most—are as follows:

1. Licensing
2. Security devices
3. Foreclosure methods
4. Interest rates
5. Pre-payment penalties
6. Balloon payments
7. Allowable fees

LET'S TAKE A CLOSER LOOK AT THESE ITEMS:

1. **Licensing:** Most states agree that "when a person acts for *compensation* in negotiating a new loan, or in selling an existing note secured by real estate, he is required to be licensed as a real estate broker or salesman." The key word here is *compensation*. A loan broker is compensated with a commission—so he must be licensed. But you, in lending only your own money, will not need a license in most cases.

   By the same token you cannot receive a commission for lending your own money.

   As I pointed out—the law could be different in your state, so check it out. In Maryland and West Virginia, for example, anyone making more than five loans per year must obtain a license from the Commissioner of Consumer Credit.

2. **Security Devices:** As I pointed out in Chapter II, your loan (promissory note) is "safe" because payment is pledged by a security device. This security device is usually a mortgage or a deed of trust. In some states, though, there are slight variations. In Minnesota your security device would be called a "contract for deed." See page 50 for a general guideline of what to expect in your state.

3. **Foreclosure Methods:** Although foreclosure methods are fairly standard when you have a deed of trust, they vary greatly with mortgages. You must find out whether you can foreclose automatically through the power of sale or whether you must go through court proceedings. Secondly comes the question of redemption period. Will there be any at all or will it be as long as one year? This information is vital and it is not difficult to obtain.

4. **Interest Rates:** Now here is an item that can make or break your investment program. In some states it can even put you in jail if you charge too much interest.

   Refer to the state by state interest rate comparison chart on page 52.

   Note how Massachusetts allows up to 18 per cent while Michigan allows only 7 per cent. I hope the folks in Michigan will forgive me for saying it—but they might as well keep their money in time certificate accounts—or ship it to a more progressive state. Low rates—like 7 and 8 per cent are indicative of a potentially sluggish real estate market because of an absence of helpful second financing.

SECURITY DEVICES USED
IN THE FIFTY STATES

Alabama	Mortgage	Montana	Deed of Trust
Arizona	Deed of Trust	Nebraska	Deed of Trust
Alaska	Deed of Trust	Nevada	Deed of Trust
Arkansas	Both	New Hamshire	Mortgage
California	Deed of Trust	New Jersey	Mortgage
Colorado	Deed of Trust	New Mexico	Deed of Trust
Connecticut	Mortgage	New York	Mortgage
Delaware	Mortgage	North Carolina	Deed of Trust
Florida	Mortgage	North Dakota	Mortgage
Georgia	Mortgage	Ohio	Mortgage
Hawaii	Mortgage	Oklahoma	Mortgage
Idaho	Deed of Trust	Oregon	Deed of Trust
Illinois	Deed of Trust	Pennsylvania	Mortgage
Indiana	Mortgage	Rhode Island	Mortgage
Iowa	Mortgage	South Carolina	Mortgage
Kansas	Mortgage	South Dakota	Mortgage
Kentucky	Both	Tennessee	Deed of Trust
Louisiana	Mortgage	Texas	Deed of Trust
Maine	Mortgage	Utah	Deed of Trust
Maryland	Both	Vermont	Mortgage
Massachusetts	Mortgage	Virginia	Deed of Trust
Michigan	Mortgage	Washington	Deed of Trust
Minnesota	Mortgage	West Virginia	Deed of Trust
Mississippi	Deed of Trust	Wisconsin	Mortgage
Missouri	Deed of Trust	Wyoming	Mortgage

NOTE:

Many states use both forms of security devices. Only the most common is listed. The states listed as "both" are either equally divided in security device usage or it is based on regional considerations.

Many states—like Maine and Utah—have a complicated sliding interest rate scale based upon consumer finance laws.

Make sure that your state doesn't have a tricky or over-burdening usury law.

5. **Prepayment Penalties:** I have stressed the importance of pre-payment penalties. They not only can increase your profits but can help to prevent bothersome quick payoffs. And without the penalty your note would be subject to greater resale discounts.

While I can assure you that most states allow prepayments, there are some exceptions. In Illinois, for instance, the current maximum interest rate is 9½ per cent but prepayment penalties are outlawed if your interest rate exceeds 8 per cent.

6. **Balloon Payments:** Where the final installment payment on a note is greater than the preceding payments and it pays the note in full, such final installment is termed a balloon payment. Thus a state law that prohibits balloon payments on loans under three years is really saying that interest only or partially amortized loans are illegal. Many states direct themselves to balloon payments—and the requirements vary greatly. So check them out.

In California, a 1974 law states that any loan originated by a licensee and secured by an owner occupied dwelling, for a term of six years or less, cannot have any installment greater than twice the amount of the smallest installment. Thus in California an owner-occupant is now often deprived of the popular "interest-only" loan. This law does not apply to purchase money loans, however.

By contrast, the state of Nevada does not have any laws prohibiting balloon payments, thus the investor and borrower are both free to select terms that are mutually acceptable.

7. **Allowable Fees:** In all 50 states you will find some type of licensing law for real property loan brokers. And you can also be sure that there are numerous laws, regulations and restrictions in regards to what fees can or cannot be charged a borrower. You would be wise to discover what these fees are and if applicable to follow the guidelines just as if you were a loan broker. But remember one thing—you cannot charge a commission or loan fee (which is often considered to be a commission).

Such costs would include appraisal, escrow, title, notary, recording and credit investigation fees. It is obvious that probably none of the above fees will ever go into your pocket. But they are allowable charges that, within legal limits, can be passed on to the borrower.

MAXIMUM CONTRACT INTEREST RATES IN THE UNITED STATES

Alabama (note 2)	Montana 10%
Arizona 10%	Nebraska 11%
Alaska (note 3)	Nevada 12%
Arkansas 10%	New Hampshire Any Rate
California 10%	New Jersey 9½%
Colorado (note 1)	New Mexico 10%
Connecticut (note 2)	New York 8½%
Delaware (note 3)	North Carolina 12%
Florida 10%	North Dakota 9%
Georgia 9%	Ohio 8%
Hawaii 12%	Oklahoma 10%
Idaho 10%	Oregon 10%
Illinois 9½%	Pennsylvania 8%
Indiana 8%	Rhode Island 15%
Iowa 9%	South Carolina 9%
Kansas 10%	South Dakota 10%
Kentucky 8½%	Tennessee 10%
Louisiana 10%	Texas 10%
Maine (note 1)	Utah (note 1)
Maryland 12%	Vermont (note 3)
Massachusetts 18%	Virginia 12%
Michigan 7%	Washington 12%
Minnesota 8%	West Virginia 8%
Mississippi 10%	Wisconsin (note 2)
Missouri 10%	Wyoming (note 1)

(1) Consumer Credit Code (No usury laws, interest rates can vary depending upon size and length of loan.)
(2) Interest rates vary according to size and length of loan.
(3) Use an add-on percentage usually added to the discount rate established by the Federal Home Loan Bank. Four per cent plus FHLB rate is common. Because of this rates can vary each calendar quarter.

APPENDIX TO INTEREST RATE CHART

COLORADO: A consumer credit code state, Colorado allows real estate loans up to 12 per cent. However, loan brokers or those regulated under the small lenders license act may charge up to 18 per cent.

HAWAII: The actual interest rate in Hawaii is 1 per cent per month, which means an annual rate of 12 per cent. A loan written for only six months, then, would be limited to 6 per cent interest.

MAINE: A consumer credit code state. Maine, which reports a strong secondary money market, allows up to 18 per cent interest on loans less than $2,500 and up to 36 per cent with larger loans. Typical rates, however, vary between 14 and 16 per cent.

MASSACHUSETTS: Not only does Massachusetts allow 18 per cent on secondary real estate loans, but most seconds are written at that amount. There is no right of redemption.

NEW HAMPSHIRE: Any interest rate goes in New Hampshire. But there is a catch — all loans must be originated by a state licensee.

UTAH: Another consumer credit code state, most secondary loans in Utah carry interest rates between 14 and 18 per cent.

CORPORATIONS: Most states allow corporations to pay higher loan rates than individuals. Occasionally you will find one of these profitable opportunities.

YOUR PREPAYMENT CHOICES

Before you lend your first dollar you should have a well defined "game plan" in mind. What are your goals and how do you intend to reach them?

In regards to loan repayment you have two opposing choices. Each one is filled with pros and cons. On one hand you can accept payment in "interest only" installments. On the other hand you can receive equal monthly payments (fully amortized) that will pay off the loan in full with the final payment. Your choice might even lie between the two. I am not going to give any advice as to which is the best way to go, but I am going to give you some criteria to use so you may make your own decision.

First, let's take a look at both a fully amortized and an interest-only loan. The example is for a $5,000 note at 10 per cent interest with a five-year due date. The remaining balance is noted at the end of each year.

Beginning Balance	Year 1	Year 2	Year 3	Year 4	Year 5
$5,000 (Interest only)	$5,000	$5,000	$5,000	$5,000	$5,000
$5,000 (Amortized)	4,188	3,292	2,302	1,208	0

Now let's take a look at the interest collected each year from the fully amortized loan as compared to the interest-only loan. These figures can be useful in helping you to decide which route to take.

	Year 1	Year 2	Year 3	Year 4	Year 5
Interest Only Loan:	$500	$500	$500	$500	$500
Fully Amortized Loan:	463	379	285	181	66

TOTAL INTEREST COLLECTED IN 5 YEARS

Interest Only Loan: $2,500

Fully Amortized Loan: $1,374

The amazing fact about these figures is that the interest is always charged against the current principal balance. With each ensuing payment the principal balance of the amortized loan declines and thus so do interest charges. During the five-year period the interest-only investor earns $1,126 more on his note than the amortized loan investor — yet both are truly earning 10 per cent on their money. In the long run both come out about equal because the amortized lender gets his money back at a faster rate so he can invest in another loan sooner. After the first year he will have collected total payments (interest and principal) of $1,274.82 vs. only $500 for the interest-only investor. Let's examine each choice further.

1. **Interest Only:** There are a lot of advantages with the interest-only loan. An important one is that they are in great demand by other investors and often by homeowners. In California, for example, this demand is not being met by the licensed loan broker. Primarily this is because of the new California Real Estate Law (Article 7; Section 10244 and 10244.1) which prohibits balloon payments and thus interest-only or partially amortized loans for owner occupants.

   For our purposes (at least in California and states with similar laws) this ruling is significant because it only applies to real estate licensees who receive a commission for arranging a loan. According to the California Department of Real Estate, a private citizen lending his own money would not be bound by this law. The area is rather "grey" but this ruling does correspond to general practice.

   Unfortunately, I feel this law hurts the borrowing public more than it helps them. The idea behind it is that a lump sum payoff would come too quickly and be too large for the average homeowner. But regardless of the reasons, this type of loan is in demand.

   For some investors, interest only loans can be ideal. For the person who comes into a great deal of cash but is in need of extra income, the interest only loan is the answer. Consider a divorcee who receives a $25,000 settlement plus $400 per month alimony. I would expect that she will not be able to get by on $400 and would be forced to nibble away at the $25,000 — until it is all gone. But enter the interest-only second! By collecting interest only she can earn an extra $200 per month (at 10 per cent) and in five years she will still have her $25,000 nest egg.

2. **Fully amortized:** One distinct advantage of the amortized loan is that you get your money back faster so you can put it out again faster. And between the "ins and outs" you can collect interest from your bank or savings.

   A second advantage of a quicker pay-back is that as the principal amount of the loan declines, your loan becomes smaller and therefore safer as the borrower's payoff balance can more easily be met. I feel that this safety feature is much more important in an area (or time) where home appreciation rates are low. If homes gain in value only 5 per cent a year you will benefit from greater loan security. If appreciation is over 12 per cent (as it generally was in the western states in 1976), I don't think the safety feature of a declining loan balance is worth "beans."

As I said before, in most states you will have the choice as to loan terms. If you want to take a middle road and accept a pay-back of 1 or 2 per cent per month, then that's okay, too.

WHERE TO FIND BORROWERS

Finding qualified borrowers sometimes reminds me of fishing. You cast your baited hook, take a few nibbles and then finally make a good catch. Sometimes it is a long wait but then every once in a while you go home with a whole string of good fish.

It's not much different than "catching" a good borrower. You might go weeks without a nibble then all of a sudden you will have two or three who are ready, willing and able.

If you take the do-it-yourself approach there are many thousands of willing borrowers, but at times it may be hard to locate them. If you invest your funds through a loan broker there will be fewer customers but they will be easier to find.

The reason for this is quite simple—the cost to a borrower is usually very high when he goes through a loan broker. Not only will he be charged an appraisal fee, title fee, etc. but he will pay the loan broker's commission, often 10 to 15 per cent of the face amount of the loan. Therefore, a borrower who needs $5,000 will find himself paying another $750 to $1,200 in charges.

The costs are steep and they eliminate many would be borrowers—especially the investor who is looking for good leverage. But on the other hand some loan brokers aren't hurting for customers because they spend a lot of dollars on advertising. I am sure you have seen an ad on television seeking out homeowners for $5,000 to $15,000 loans.

There are many ways to find borrowers, but let's discuss only the two major techniques. They are simple as well as effective. The first method is to place an advertisement in your local newspaper. The second technique is to contact local real estate brokers.

I placed the following ad in my local newspaper of 40,000 circulation. Results were not spectacular but more than adequate as I received six calls. It turned out that all six were acceptable as potential borrowers. The only problem was that I did not have enough capital to help all six. My ad, which ran only two days at a cost of $7, read as follows:

MONEY TO LEND—Private investor has $$money for qualified homeowners. Repay 10% interest only with five-year due date. No commission or unnecessary charges. Call 689-5090 Monday thru Wednesday from 10 a.m. to 2 p.m.

The second method of finding clients is to contact several local real estate brokers. I can guarantee you that they are always looking for second money to put together a sale. And often the Realtor comes in contact with a holder of a purchase money note that is looking for quick cash.

The Realtor will most likely welcome your source of funds. He will be glad to introduce you to a client who needs a second so he can consummate a sale and earn his regular commission. Most Realtors will not ask for a commission on your transaction because they will only be referring or introducing you to their clients. If one does ask—just simply tell him to "forget it" and go on to the next office. You are doing him a bigger favor than he will be doing you. I estimate that my firm of 14 salespersons would earn an extra $20,000 to $25,000 in yearly commissions if we had an unending flow of second money available.

QUESTIONS TO ASK YOUR BORROWER

After you get a nibble from a prospective borrower, ask him the following questions. If his answers are favorable and fit your requirements, then move on to the second stage. Let's take a look at this "interview checklist."

1. For what purposes do you need a loan?
2. How much money do you need?
3. Where are you employed?
4. What is your income?
5. What is your property address?
6. What do you consider your property worth?
7. What is the amount of your "first" loan?
8. What are the amounts of any other loans or liens on your home?
9. How long have you owned your home?

10. What is the age of your home?
11. What is the size of your lot?
12. What is the size of your home?
13. In what condition is the property?
14. What is the condition of the neighborhood?
15. How much can you afford on monthly loan payments?
16. How long do you need the loan for?
17. Are all your home payments and property taxes current?
18. What is your phone number?

Start with question number one and work down to the last. If at any time you receive an answer you don't like then politely end your interview by saying "thank you very much but your situation doesn't meet my requirements." For instance, his equity might be too small, his home too old or his income inadequate. If you like his answers, though, then take his phone number and make arrangements to personally meet with him at his property. At the next meeting you would inspect his home and button down the tentative terms of your second, subject to a favorable credit report, property appraisal and preliminary title search.

BORROWER QUALIFICATIONS

The security for your loan of course lies with the promissory note combined with either a mortgage or deed of trust. "So what does it matter whether or not my borrower has lousy credit? I can always foreclose!"

To a point this often asked question makes sense. But we must look beyond the obvious. There are two negative situations you should try to avoid and one positive situation you should try to create.

The negative situation is a borrower who is constantly late or one who bounces every other check. Although this borrower may never force you to file for foreclosure, he will keep you on the brink of doing so. The second negative situation is the foreclosure itself— an extra problem which seldom results in any real extra benefits.

A positive goal to strive for is a reliable borrower who will add strength to your note in the event you ever put it on the open market.

While no checklist or pre-qualification will guarantee a good borrower, they will, however, help to weed out some undesirables from the start.

Going back to the checklist on page 57, pay particular attention to items 1 thru 4 plus 8 and 17.

If your prospective borrower needs a loan because he is having money problems (question #1) then this is a "red flag." Pay special attention to the remaining key questions.

For instance he may need money (don't we all at times) and yet have a good job and income. Thus far the prospect would be a good risk. On the other hand, though, he may need money because he lost his job and is $3,000 in debt. This is a second "red flag." But he still may be a good prospect if he either 1) has a good chance of landing a new job; 2) has a clean credit background and 3) has sufficient equity in his property. All factors must be considered.

You might even be faced with a situation in which your prospect is hopelessly out of work (question 3), has no extra income source (question 4) and is two months behind in his first loan payments (question 17). The situation looks hopeless but all is not lost if you are willing to consider a short term loan with a healthy prepayment penalty. This would depend of course on the value of the property and the amount of the equity. In addition you should insist that the property be listed for sale at a realistic price with a responsible Realtor.

The above described prospect is obviously in a losing battle — he is losing his home. Most people I have known in this situation will attempt to sell their property to salvage what they have left. If he is willing to sell, then you might consider this prospect reliable enough for a short term loan.

Borrower qualifications are important. And although you can usually rely upon your interview plus a preliminary title search to give you a good idea of what you're getting into, I suggest going one step further. Obtain a credit report for each prospect. If you don't have access to a credit bureau then apply for membership. It isn't very expensive and some day it will pay off.

PROPERTY QUALIFICATIONS

If your prospective borrower checks out grade A — then you're halfway home. But just as important as the borrower is the property itself. Pay close attention to "interview checklist" items 5, 6, 10, 13 and 14.

If the property is old, run down and in a bad neighborhood then I suggest you forget the loan no matter how good the buyer's personal history and credit rating is. It would be considered a "high risk" loan and the only justification for taking such a loan would be if the equity to value ratio was very high. For instance a $30,000 market value with only a $10,000 first loan plus your second of $5,000.

Whenever you are considering a borderline property, I suggest you call one or two local Realtors who are active in residential resales. Ask them what the situation is in the "questionable" neighborhood. Find out if properties are selling and appreciating as fast as they are in surrounding areas.

Beware of homes that are in a transitional zoning area (like changing from residential to multiple or commercial). Try to avoid homes that have converted a garage into a bedroom or family room or that are adjacent to a busy street or commercial zone.

FOUR WAYS TO APPRAISE PROPERTY

A lot of checklist questions will not be fully answered until the subject property is appraised. Here are four easy and different methods the do-it-yourself lender can utilize to get the job done.

● *Don't Do It:* What may sound like a smart-aleck answer really isn't. I think you are wasting your time or the borrower's money if you appraise a home with an obvious high equity. An example would be a home in a quality neighborhood (values ranging between $50,000 and $70,000) with a first loan of only $20,000. Your preliminary title search will confirm the approximate amount of first loan and a visual inspection will satisfy you as to condition and relative value of the home. But this short-cut procedure will be the exception rather than the rule.

● *Hire Fee Appraiser*: Whenever faced with a difficult property to valuate or on a borderline situation in regards to amount of equity, then call in a professional appraiser. The fee —which will probably range from $50 to $150—can properly be charged to the borrower.

I don't suggest you call a Realtor for what is commonly called an opinion of market value. This is not an appraisal but an estimate of what the particular salesman thinks the home would sell for on the open market. Two different Realtors can often vary their opinions by as much as $2,000 or $3,000. Hire only a certified appraiser.

● *Use Existing Appraisal:* Often your second loan will be placed on a property in conjunction with a new first loan. In this case you can rely on the appraisal made by the bank or savings and loan. In many areas of our country 80-10-10 loans are quite popular. This means a new loan of 80 per cent of the appraised value plus a 10 per cent second. It's all handled with one appraisal and in one escrow.

You might also be faced with a situation where a borrower has just purchased or refinanced his home and he can supply you with the recent appraisal.

● *Do-It-Yourself:* This method is best for tract subdivisions with lots of similar homes. I don't recommend it when you are faced with a "one-of-a-kind" property. Those are best left to a fee appraiser.

This method establishes a market value for the property in much the same manner a Realtor would use, by comparing sale prices of similar homes. In fact, if you are working with a reliable Realtor you might ask him to do it.

Start your market value appraisal by inspecting the layout and condition of the subject property. Remember, you can't compare apples to oranges. So if the property has three bedrooms, two baths and a 250-square-foot family room then this becomes your basic criteria when comparing it to other homes. If the home badly needs inside painting then estimate the expense (say $400). If the garage door is hanging by its hinges then estimate the cost of repair. (Let's use $500.) For the sake of example let's assume the home you are appraising is in good to excellent condition except for the two above-noted items which total $900.

Next comes the hard part. You must now locate three similar homes (three bedrooms, two baths plus a small family room) that have sold within the last five or six months. Don't use anything older than six months unless you add to their value because of appreciation. These three homes should be in the same subdivision as your subject property.

Often you can find three comparables by driving the neighborhood and looking for "sold" signs. If this doesn't do it then ask a few people in the neighborhood if they know of any homes which were recently sold. If you still don't have three then ask at the closest real estate office.

After you get a list of three or more homes then drive by and make a street inspection. It would be even better to ring the doorbell and ask if you could make a fast inspection of the home, although this isn't necessary as long as you are convinced you have the correct facts (number of bedrooms, sales price, etc.).

Once this is done find the average sales price for the properties. Selling prices of $35,000, $36,000 and $36,500 would indicate an approximate value of $35,833. But give yourself some leeway because, as I said earlier, most market analyses are not accurate.

Your final step would be to subtract $900 (cost of painting and garage door) from the estimated value of $35,833. Of course, this penalty only has meaning if you are assured the other three properties were in near-perfect condition. By the same token, if your subject home has an extra (built-in electric kitchen) the others do not have then you would have to add an approximate value (about 50 per cent of the original cost) to your appraisal.

As I am sure you now realize, this fourth method of appraising is often haphazard and should only be used when there is absolutely no problem with equity and loan ratios.

HOW MUCH BORROWER
EQUITY IS REALLY NECESSARY??

One of the most important questions which you must ask yourself is "how much equity should a borrower have in his home?" There is no simple answer to this question. Your decision must be based upon all the facts and figures which you have thus far accumulated from your first interview and property appraisal.

As a general guideline, I have never heard of a loan broker lending any amount which would exceed 80 per cent of the property value. And some will not go beyond 75 per cent.

But when you are "doing-it-yourself" there is a different set of rules for the ball game. Many fine opportunties that are passed up by loan brokers will become available to you.

Always keeping in mind that it's the borrower's equity that is really pledged for the security of your loan, you should make your final decision based upon five factors. They are: property value based on appraisal; existing liens and encumbrances; protection costs for your loan; selling costs of the property; and existing market conditions.

1. *Property value based on appraisal:* Although you and the borrower may have a rough idea as to value, only a formal appraisal will give you the firm figure which you will need to make your "equity" decision. This appraisal figure will be vitally important when you are working with either a short equity situation or an unusual property.

2. *Existing liens and incumbrances:* These would include all loans or debts which have been recorded against the property and therefore would be ahead of your second. They can be determined by a preliminary title search plus a statement of condition (current balance of the existing loan). If you are using the services of a title company both the preliminary and statement would be obtained during an escrow period.

After receiving the dollar amounts from the first two factors, you will have the basic information needed before going on to step 3. For demonstration purposes let's use an example with a $40,000 appraised value and liens and encumbrances totalling $25,000. This home has an apparent equity of $15,000 or 37.5 per cent. While on the surface it appears that this is enough equity, we must further whittle down this percentage to arrive at a "secure" loan position.

3. *Protection Costs for Your Loan:* You must consider how much it will cost if the loan goes into default and you have to dig into your pocket to protect it. As a safe guideline, you should allow for seven months (four for foreclosure and three to sell the property) worth of house payments.

The costs would include first loan payments, monthly pro-rated tax and insurance payments plus foreclosure charges. Continuing with the above example, the borrower's $40,000 home payments would be approximately $210 per month (x7=$1,470) plus monthly tax and insurance payments of $75 (x7=$525) plus foreclosure charges of $250. The grand total, which comes to $2,245, should be deducted from the $15,000 equity, leaving a more realistic figure of $12,755.

4. *Selling costs of the property:* In order to compute selling costs, you first must establish what type of first loan the property has and whether or not it contains a prepayment penalty. Government insured loans (FHA or VA) do not contain pre-payment clauses while most conventional loans do have penalties. It is most common for the penalties to call for six month's interest. Using our example of a $25,000 loan, I'll estimate this cost at $1,150 for our purposes.

Secondly, we must consider the actual selling costs which would include a Realtor's commission of 6 or 7 per cent and any possible loan discount points required to place a new FHA or VA loan. I would only consider points as an expense when the subject property is in an FHA or VA resale market. If the home is over $50,000 or in a neighborhood that traditionally has few government insured sales, then I would ignore them. Incidentally, each point represents 1 per cent of the buyer's new loan and, because they can vary between 1 to 7 at any given time, they are very difficult to properly assess as a selling expense item. For our continuing example I am using a 6 per cent commission ($2,400) based upon a $40,000 sale price.

A third selling cost item to include is an amount to cover any necessary repairs or painting. I usually use $500 as a starting point. But when you first inspect the home if you find that $500 would not cover the present conditions, then raise the figure to whatever may be required.

So far we have selling expenses of $1,150 for pre-payment penalty, $2,400 for commission and $500 for upkeep. A total of $4,050 which must be subtracted from the remaining equity position of $12,755. Our new total is now $8,705. This figure represents what you could safely lend to the borrower. With this example you would require the borrower to have nearly 16 per cent of his own equity in the home. The loan amounts would thus total 84 per cent. But hold onto your hat as there is one more important consideration.

5. *Existing Market Conditions:* So far all the computations have been based on present values and property conditions. But what would happen if the borrower nearly destroys the house in the next five years? What happens if the home loses value in the next five years? I'll give you a fast answer to the first question and a lengthy one to the last.

People don't usually change too much from one year to the next. If the home is well cared for on your first inspection then it probably will be five years later. If it is going to be wrecked, you will see it happening before your eyes. If that possibility seems real then don't make the loan. It's not worth the worry.

A real concern would be if real estate values went on downward declines as does the stock market. Your loan could be wiped out one month and then mysteriously resurrected the next. But fortunately this is not the case. Home values are —and always have been —on the rise. It's called appreciation and it's largely a result of inflation as evidenced by the rising consumer price index described in Chapter I.

According to a report from the research and economic department of the National Association of Realtors, home prices continue to move up, particularly in the West, where a 16.9 per cent increase has been recorded over the past 12 months through September 1976. The North Central region by contrast, has experienced a 9.2 per cent jump, while increases in the Northeast and South regions have been 5.1 and 4.9 per cent respectively. The report goes on to say that the national average for 1976 should be about 8 per cent.

While this is a sizable increase, it is below the 10.4 per cent rise in 1975 and the 10.9 figure in 1974.

Rising prices bring greater security for your loans. If the $40,000 home used in our example is in the West, by all conservative expectations it should average 10 per cent appreciation per year for the next five years. This would mean a value of $64,420—thus the borrower's equity (and your security) would increase by $24,420. Not Bad! But don't get excited because your considerations are more complicated.

Because you have no guarantee that the borrower won't default on your loan after just one year or even six months, you cannot realistically plan on five years' appreciation. I recommend that you rely only on six months' appreciation. And be conservative—use 10 per cent in the West, 6 per cent in the North Central region, and just 3.5 per cent in the Northeast and Southern areas. Each year you will want to review and perhaps change these percentages. And these percentages will have even more meaning if you convert them to your actual city or county appreciation rates.

Prior to discussing market conditions, it was decided that the borrower in our example would receive an $8,705 loan. But because of market conditions, if you so desire, you can (in the West) add a six-month "appreciation factor" of $2,000 to the amount of the loan.

This would bring the potential loan to $10,705 and more importantly would allow you to lend the difference between the first loan and $35,705 (which nearly equals 90 per cent of the value of the property). In other regions, of course, your "appreciation factor" would be less so you would not arrive at as high a loan figure.

Just in case I have lost you, here is a recap:

Appraised Value: $40,000

Minus:	Existing loans . . .	$25,000
	Loan protections costs	2,245
	Selling costs	+ 4,050

$31,295

−$31,295

8,705

Plus: "Appreciation Factor" . . . . . + 2,000

Equals allowable loan amount: $10,705

90 PER CENT LOAN OPPORTUNITIES

Once you begin to actively seek loan opportunities, I am sure that you will find a lot of potential borrowers wanting 90 per cent loans (10 per cent borrower equity).

There are three simple explanations of why this is so. First of all the vast majority of loan brokers will not go beyond combined encumbrances of 80 per cent. Therefore many good customers are turned away.

The second reason is that the majority of clients referred by Realtors will be owner-occupant home buyers who need a 10 per cent second to go along with their 10 per cent down payment. These buyers are usually well qualified and reliable but a little short on cash. They are not minimum down buyers but "conventional loan" buyers who are most likely buying a better than average property.

These home buyers could probably qualify for 90 per cent conventional loans but would pay higher interest rates and loan origination fees. Their best bet is often an 80 per cent conventional loan along with a second. Believe me, as a Realtor with over 11 years experience, there are many sensible reasons why home buyers SHOULD use secondary financing when available.

Thirdly, just as the Realtor refers many owner-occupant home buyers he will also be an excellent source for property investors. Many of these investors are looking for leverage which requires as small a down payment as possible. These are often very substantial people who will never pay the high loan fee required by loan brokers. A little later I'll give you an excellent technique for dealing with investors.

When you create your own loan portfolio, you are the boss. You can avoid all 90 per cent loans or you can select only those that make sense. But I caution you to never exceed 90 per cent with combined loans. Always insist (even with purchase money loans) that your borrower have a minimum of 10 per cent equity.

As an added precaution you might want to limit those borrowers that are consolidating debts to an 80 per cent maximum. Many have already had a history of problems and therefore are the most likely candidates for future ones.

INVESTOR OPPORTUNITIES

For the do-it-yourself lender an investor client can be your biggest bonanza. He usually is not in debt and often has a net worth of more than $50,000! Because he is not an owner-occupant an interest-only loan will probably not be limited or outlawed by archaic state laws. And as your loan customer, you will become familiar with the investor's requirements and payment habits. This should lead to a relationship that will produce many excellent loans.

In my first book, "The Monopoly Game," I outline a conservative program where an investor in single family homes can start on a shoe-string and end up after 11 years with eight or more properties and a net worth of nearly $300,000. But for many investors this time schedule would be an impossibility without second money.

When dealing with real property investors, a unique opportunity opens up. And that is a blanket mortgage or deed of trust. It is handled in the following way:

An investor asks for a 90 per cent loan but you feel the total situation does not justify it. You can counter by suggesting a promissory note secured by two deeds of trust (or mortgages). One would be secured by the property the investor is buying and the second would be secured by either his home or another property. This is the basic idea although you will find some variations between title companies and states.

In the event of default, you can foreclose first on the rental and if not enough money is received to cover your loan you can then proceed against the residence or another rental property. By using this technique you should never have to say no to a qualified investor.

VI

The Loan Broker
Approach

The do-it-yourself approach to secondary financing can be both monetarily rewarding and a lot of fun. I know of several investors who manage their own portfolios and are making a great deal of money.

Even though it can be a successful venture, "doing it on your own" is not for everyone. It takes time and a degree of specialized knowledge. Not only must you learn the basic facts presented in this book but you must acquire a complete understanding of the laws in your state and the market conditions of real property in your locale.

For these basic reasons, many thousands of investors across the country use the services of licensed loan brokers. And almost without exception, the investor can make as much money using the loan brokers' services as he can on his own.

One important reason for this is that the loan broker, unlike other investment brokers, does not charge the investor a commission. His commission is paid by the borrower. In most states the size of his commission is regulated by law. In California for instance, the law limits a broker's commission on second trust deeds to 5 per cent of the principal on a loan of less than two years; 10 per cent of the principal on loans between two and three years and 15 per cent of the principal on a loan of three years or more. Thus on a three-year, $5,000 loan, a broker can earn a commission of $750. But your net profit return will be the same as if you created and managed the entire loan.

PROFILE OF A LOAN BROKER

Loan brokers can be found in small "one-man" offices or in large firms with 20 or 30 branch offices. Most common, however, are the relatively small companies with just two or three people.

Incidentally, secondary loan brokers are often confused with mortgage loan brokers. A mortgage broker is usually one who specializes in first loans. He represents large investor combines or small savings and loans, which put their money into the FHA-VA or conventional money market. The mortgage loan broker is in direct competition with banks and large savings and loans.

In looking through the yellow pages for a secondary loan broker, you will probably be faced with this confusion. If the ad does not specifically mention "seconds" or "homeowner loans" the firm is in the "first" loan business rather than into "seconds."

A loan broker is licensed by the state in which he conducts his business. He has a great deal of general knowledge of the practices and conditions of the local real estate sales market. He is an expert in real estate law, finance and appraising. And he is proficient in servicing your loan from beginning to end.

In short, he is a "pro" you can usually rely on to handle your investment portfolio from beginning to end. All you need to do is let him go to work for you — and you can then sit back and bank your monthly profits.

SELECTING YOUR LOAN

When using a loan broker's services, you don't just hand him $10,000 and say "go to work." What you do is select a loan that he has already negotiated and probably consummated with funds made available to him.

This is called "warehousing." Because a person cannot lend his own money and receive a commission, the broker must borrow short-term funds from a third party. When the loan is sold the broker then returns the money to the "warehouse" where he has his line of credit.

Like any other business, many loan brokers are going to have "favorite" customers. There is a better than even chance that the favored clients will get first chance at the best loans. For this reason you are likely to be in an inferior position if you are a new customer with only enough funds for one or two loans.

Although I trust the ethics of the vast majority of loan brokers, human nature is human nature. It is possible that a loan broker will have made a bad loan which he has not been able to peddle for six months. And then you —a new customer —comes into his office with $10,000 and all the eagerness of a frisky puppy. The stage has been set! And an unethical broker would try to sell you on the merits of his "white elephant" loan.

I don't mean to scare you off. But I want to give you two basic facts which you must keep in mind. First of all find out as much as possible about the firm you plan to deal with. And don't let them know you have only $5,000 to invest. It certainly won't hurt your position if they think you have $50,000 to put out.

Secondly, you must be armed with enough knowledge about seconds and your local real estate market so that you can separate good buys from bad buys, if necessary, without the broker's advice. So by using these two techniques you will not only look like an intelligent investor but you *will be one also*.

Many brokers may provide you with printed or mimeographed information on all of their available loans. Sometimes there might be 20 or more offerings and in some cases only four or five. Often a broker has only a few loans to sell because he either is in a slow market period, has a healthy surplus of investors to immediately buy his loans, or is not too active in seeking new loans.

If you are only offered a selection of four or five loans, then ask why. If you decide that it's because the loan broker is not active in his field, then you probably should go to another broker who might be more competitive. But let me caution you on one point. You should find a healthy "second" market in an active high interest state like Nevada. But if you are looking for seconds in a state like North Dakota, you might not even find a loan broker let alone one with four or five loans to sell. Only compare apples to apples! In other words compare two or three brokers in your home area.

On the next two pages there is a sample of typical loan offerings by an active loan broker. Note the variety of each loan. No mention of interest rates is made in the offering —that is because each loan is at legal maximum rate unless noted otherwise.

YOU GET MORE THAN MEETS THE EYE

Most state laws prohibit or limit many would-be creative practices of loan brokers. One very common area for restrictions is in the field of advertising.

In many areas a loan broker cannot advertise that he will "guarantee" to buy back any bad loans which he might have sold you.

SAMPLE OF TYPICAL LOAN OFFERINGS

Appraised Value	Prior Lien	Equity	Amount of Our Loan	Our Loan % of Equity
$50,000	$32,250	$17,750	$8,000	45%
$36,500	$18,800	$17,700	$9,000	51%
$28,000	$18,000	$10,000	$4,500	45%
$29,000	$12,400	$16,000	$9,500	57%
$18,000	0	$18,000	$6,700	37%
$44,000	$21,600	$22,400	$9,300	42%
$40,500	0	$40,500	$26,700	66%
$46,000	$24,100	$21,900	$10,500	48%
$50,000	$26,500	$23,500	$6,000	26%
$46,000	$32,000	$12,000	$5,000	42%
$23,000	$10,000	$13,000	$5,700	44%

SAMPLE OF TYPICAL LOAN OFFERINGS

Terms	Collateral	Time at Residence	Purpose of Loan
5 year amortized payments $177.95	Owner occupied single family residence	2 years	Pay-off purchase money second
5 year amortized payments $200.20	Owner occupied single family residence	10 years	Expand business
5 year amortized payments $100.10	Owner occupied single family residence	5 years	Debt consolidation
5 year amortized payments $211.32	Owner occupied single family residence	15 years	Purchase property for daughter
10 year amortized payments $99.20	Mobile home lot	——	Purchase money first mortgage
5 year amortized payments $206.87	Owner occupied single family residence	7 years	Buy new car ('75 Chrysler)
4 year interest only payments $276.00	Two improved mobile home lots	10 years	Business operating expenses
5 year amortized payments $233.57	Owner occupied single family residence	10 years	Purchase business equipment
5 year amortized payments $133.47	Owner occupied single family residence	——	Business expansion
5 year amortized payments $111.22	Owner occupied single family residence	3 years	Purchase business equipment
5 year amortized payments $126.79	Owner occupied single family residence	13 years	Home improvement

But most brokers do make this guarantee — and it's certainly nice to get such an offer.

Brokers are often forbidden to advertise or promise a greater return for the investor than what is their states's maximum interest rate. But due to pre-payment penalties, of which either all or a portion are returned to the investor, actual yields run about 2 per cent more than the top legal interest rates. For instance, if you live in a 10 per cent state you can expect your actual rate of return to be closer to 12 per cent — and this is before even considering a portion of discounted notes in your portfolio.

PROS AND CONS OF
USING A LOAN BROKER

On the positive side, there are many excellent reasons why you may want to use the services of a loan broker. To avoid repetition I'll state it in simple terms: They know more than you do about secondary financing; they have greater access to borrowers; they can handle your loan completely from beginning to end for a small fee which the borrower usually pays; and they often guarantee your loan.

After establishing a relationship with a loan broker it can be as simple as receiving a phone call when a good loan is available. You send a check, sign "assignment documents" (See Chapter VII) and then simply sit back and wait for your first payment. All of the leg work, the credit investigation and the property appraisal is taken care of by the broker.

And as a side benefit many loan brokers will "guarantee" your loan. If it turns out to be a bad one they will buy it back if you so desire. Many will also advance monthly payments when a borrower is late. This can be an excellent feature for a retired individual living on a tight budget.

There are also some solid reasons on the negative side of the fence. If you are the "do-it-yourself" type of person who gets a lot of satisfaction from starting and completing a well done job — then these reasons might sway you against using the loan broker.

Basically there are two reasons why it may not pay to use a loan broker. The first is that because of often restrictive laws or high loan costs many super-qualified borrowers do not use loan brokers. These borrowers are often investors themselves looking for money for real property transactions. This situation creates a legitimate market for the do-it-yourself lender.

The second reason is that some brokers, even though a small percentage, will either keep the best loans for themselves or give them to their favorite investors. These are often not new loans but ones purchased at a big discount. And needless to say, if you are not a "favorite," you may not get your share of them. These problems can best be illustrated by using my home territory —Contra Costa County in Northern California —as an example.

In the suburban areas of the county there are over 200,000 people. Almost one of every six homeowners there has a second deed of trust against their property. That makes for a lot of seconds but it has also brought a lot of loan brokers into a highly competitive market.

The average home value is about $65,000. It is a wealthy community by most standards. Because of available money there are hundreds of "second" investors in Contra Costa County that are competing with one another for loans. Because of this competitive market, most loan brokers here do not have more than four or five loans available for sale at any given time. Their biggest problem is not a lack of investors but a lack of borrowers. Thus many investors originate their own loans so they can have a wider selection or a chance at a good discount when one comes along. And as I said before, these do-it-yourself lenders have found a virtual bonanza with many qualified property investors.

But whichever road you choose to take —the decision is yours. And there is nothing stopping you from both originating loans and using a loan broker's services. Weigh the facts, and get started.

If you live in a state which has low interest rates and little or no second money activity, then you are almost forced to use an out-of-state loan broker if you decide to invest. Here are some hints on finding a good one.

FINDING A QUALIFIED LOAN BROKER

Locating a good loan broker in your community doesn't pose too much of a problem as you can easily confer with local bankers, Realtors and friends. So for the sake of explanation —I'll do it the hard way by assuming you are looking for an out-of-state broker.

Start by picking a state which has high interest rates, a growing population, and uses either the deed of trust or a mortgage without the right of redemption. Your second step would be to visit a large enough library that has a collection of United States telephone books. Select one or two communities— preferably suburban —and find at least three of the most attractive advertisements. You will most likely find them in the yellow pages listed under "Real Estate Loans." Your key is to look for the words "2nd mortgages" or "homeowner loans."

After jotting down all the information found in the ad, either write or telephone the firms and ask them the following questions:

1. Are you interested in new investors?
2. How many employees does your firm have?
3. Do you have any branch offices? How many?
4. Are you regulated and examined by a state agency? Which one?
5. How many loans do you now have available for purchase?
6. Are the loans at the highest allowable interest rate?
7. Are these loans interest only, fully amortized or various combinations?
8. What is your lending formula? What is the minimum amount of equity you require your borrower to have in his property?
9. Who appraises the property?
10. Do you guarantee your loans?
11. How do you service any loans which I might purchase?
12. Would you furnish me with the names, addresses and phone numbers of two of your investor clients, your banker and one of your creditors?

The answers to these questions will give you a fairly good idea of what type of person and firm you may be dealing with. A lot can be learned from a five-minute telephone interview. You will find out whether or not they are friendly, business-like, efficient, cooperative and eager for new business.

Incidentally, I recommend using the telephone for the dozen or so contacts you will be making. Even from Maine to California your bill will only be about $60 to $80. Not only is the telephone faster but you will usually get a lot more information and insight.

After talking with three companies I suggest you eliminate the one which seems least promising and concentrate on the other two. Now call the state regulatory body (it may be the Department of Real Estate or Insurance or Banking) and ask them if they can pass on any good or bad recommendations. Ask them if either of the loan brokers has ever had their license suspended and if so why.

Next make phone calls to the customers, bankers and creditors. But don't really expect anything very critical to come from these calls as they could all be personal friends. They still are important, though, as they will contribute to the over-all picture you are looking for.

Your last call should be to one or two Realtors in the same general area as the loan brokers. Ask if they know Mr. X and if they consider him to run an efficient and reliable business. Odds are that the Realtor will know of Mr. X and can be very helpful to you.

After you complete your calls, select what appears to be the best loan broker. Don't send him any money, however, until he sends you assignment documents or loan papers for your signature. These must be notarized in your home state and then sent to the broker along with your check.

I also recommend that you start out slow. Try just one loan at first until you are convinced the broker will live up to all of his promises in an efficient manner.

VII

Buying Seconds
at Discounts

Selling junior liens is a lot like selling used automobiles. If every part of the car is in perfect order and if the mileage is reasonably low then you can expect to receive the "low blue book" price allowed for your make and model. But if your car does not have power brakes or if it is in need of a tune-up then you may not get top dollar. You will be forced to sell at a discounted price.

In many ways you can relate the sale of seconds to sales of used automobiles. If you have a "perfect" second in all respects then you have an excellent chance of selling it for either a very small discount or perhaps none at all.

But if your note calls for 9 per cent interest when your state allows 10 per cent, then you are going to have to take a discount in order to sell. Admittedly it is more complicated than this description. But it does illustrate the most important fact about discounts. SECONDS ARE PRIMARILY DISCOUNTED IN ORDER TO BRING THE YIELD UP TO PAR AND THUS MAKE IT AN ATTRACTIVE BUY FOR THE INVESTOR.

A second but related reason junior liens are discounted has to do with the market place and market conditions. I'll have a lot more to say about this later. But the important thing to remember now is that because of market conditions plus risk factors many seconds are discounted at a far greater percentage than is necessary to "bring the yield up to par." Thus many investors make a substantial profit.

BUYING BY ASSIGNMENT

Discount purchase opportunities are numerous largely because of the ease in which a deed of trust or mortgage can be "assigned" from the original holder to a second party for cash or any other valuable consideration. This feature makes a second an easily convertible item.

When selling or buying a deed of trust, you only need to sign a standardized "assignment of deed of trust" and "endorsement of promissory note." These forms are then notarized and recorded by the trustee or a title company. Because the deed of trust is the lender's personal property, he may sell it or not for whatever price he can get. Thus the borrower or trustee has no say in the terms of the assignment.

The above process is basically the same when you are dealing with a mortgage. Only the document is called "assignment of mortgage."

POOR TERMS MAKE FOR LARGER DISCOUNTS

When the terms of your note and junior lien are weak, then you can expect to pay a larger discount when selling. In the preceding pages, I have gone over many of the basic elements that you need to "put into" your second so that it is as "discount-proof as possible in the event that you must ever sell. As we cannot fully blueprint our future, strong terms are a good defensive measure to protect your long-term investment.

Incidentally, if you ever find yourself in a position needing cash, explore the possibilities of using your seconds as collateral for a bank loan. It is often possible to arrange a loan for up to 70 per cent of the face value of your notes.

A promissory note with a low interest rate secured by a mortgage or deed of trust on a sub-par home certainly will need a "fat" discount to sell on the open market. For the liquidating investor this can mean a loss. But for the investor seeking an opportunity this can mean a bonanza.

It is generally considered that the poorer the terms or security of a second are the greater the discount will be. This is because the risk factor increases. But many seasoned investors are not afraid of the risk factor. They simply take the greater risk and buy seconds at a discount that will add to their profits. For instance a five-year note at 7 per cent with a 1 per cent monthly payback that is sold for a 22 per cent discount will increase its yield to 14 per cent. Not bad use of a 7 per cent note!

DISCOUNTING FACTORS

There is no easy answer to the question: "What situations produce a greater discount?" It's often a combination of the following 10 factors. Let's take a closer look. Then you'll understand the difficulties involved in arriving at a fair discount when either buying or selling.

1. **Market Conditions:** The good old American free enterprise system is based upon competition and the law of supply and demand. So it is with the open market for junior liens.

When there are few loans available at the "discount market," the percentages will be in favor of the seller. And this is often the case when real estate sales are booming, employment is full and interest rates are low.

But when the economy turns sluggish there is usually a surplus of loans available and thus the discounts are larger. Therefore, in most communities a loan might be discounted only 10 per cent in a "boom" year. But the same loan might go for a 20 per cent discount in a sluggish year.

2. **Purchase Money Loans:** As I said earlier, there is nothing wrong with a properly drawn and secured purchase money loan. If it meets all the standard criteria, this loan can stand up just as well in the discount market as a hard money loan.

However, this is often not the case. Loan brokers and investors are highly suspicious of purchase money loans because they are historically bad. This is because a lot of anxious real estate agents and frustrated sellers will put together a piece of junk and call it a purchase money second. Their main purpose is to sell the property and not to create a solid second.

The terms, for instance, may call for only 6 per cent interest in a 10 per cent market. This means the seller (holder of the purchase money loan) will possibly have to pay a 50 per cent discount when he goes to sell.

With purchase money loans it is important to evaluate each one independently and pay particular attention to the value of the security. In other words, is the subject home truly worth x dollars and does the property contain the right amount of equity to secure the loan?

3. **Hard Money Loans:** Because hard money loans are usually originated by a loan broker or an experienced investor and because the subject property usually has sufficient protective equity, these

loans are in a favorite position. They will normally be subjected to a smaller discount than most purchase money loans because the risk factor is smaller.

4. **Yield:** By yield I mean the yearly profit percentage the loan repays. If you are in a 12 per cent market then discounting is required to at least bring a note yield up to 12 per cent.

Thus by increasing the discount of a note you are able to bring the yield up to par (normal interest rate for your area) or to even increase its yield beyond the norm so that an extra profit can be taken by the investor.

This extra profit is not considered to be usurious if it is clear that the investor takes the loan on assignment from another lender. It can then be shown that the first lender loses the discount and not the borrower.

5. **Payback and Duration:** The monthly payback and duration of the loan are as crucial as the amount of interest in determining what the true yield will be with the discount. The actual rate of interest goes up with a shorter remaining term of the loan. And the larger the note payback the higher the face interest.

The following examples will show what I mean: On a $1,000, 10 per cent note with an interest-only payback an investor will receive $500 in interest over a five-year period. Discounting the note by 10 per cent will give the investor another $100 to add to his $500. Five years divided into the total return of $600 brings a yearly yield of 12 per cent. If the note is discounted by 20 per cent the yield increases to 14 per cent per annum.

However, take the same note and reduce it to a two-year duration with a 10 per cent discount. It now brings a 15 per cent yield, and a 20 per cent discount creates a 20 per cent yield. So the shorter the duration is the higher the yield will be when you use the same discount percentage.

An increase in yield is also realized as the payback increases. For instance, a 9 per cent note with a three-year due date that has been discounted 25 per cent would yield approximately 22 per cent with a 1½ per cent payback and 24 per cent with a 2 per cent payback.

The following table will give you an idea about discounting effects. It is based on a five-year due date with a 1 per cent monthly payback. It shows what discount percentages must be used to realize a 15 per cent yield on loans with a face value from 7 to 11 per cent.

ORIGINAL LOAN	NECESSARY DISCOUNT	=	YIELD
7%	24.67%		15%
8%	22.13%		15%
9%	19.46%		15%
10%	16.63%		15%
11%	13.65%		15%

Understanding as well as determining discounts and yield percentages can be difficult. This task can be made a lot easier if you obtain the "Realty Bluebook" from Professional Publishing Corp., P.O. Box 4187, San Rafael, California 94903. The price is $12 plus 6 per cent sales tax for California residents. It contains approximately 400 pages of tables, tax effects and contract clauses. The table includes: yields for discounted mortgages; amortization; remaining balance; proration; factors to compute monthly interest plus many others that will make life much easier for the do-it-yourself lender.

6. **Pre-Payment and Late Charges:** The discount amount is also determined by how complete the loan is. If the loan does not contain a pre-payment clause, for instance, a larger discount will be necessary. The reason is simple. A note with a pre-payment clause has the potential of increasing an investor's interest return by as much as 100 per cent. For instance, a 10 per cent interest-only loan calling for a six-month interest penalty for early pay-off will produce a 20 per cent yield if paid off in six months. The effects of an early pay-off can actually double the investor's return. Even after two years a prepayment penalty with the above example will increase the investor's actual return from 10 to 12½ per cent. And most loans are paid off before maturity.

A late charge is important for two reasons. It encourages the borrower to make his payments on time and secondly it can increase the yield of a loan by a small amount when enough payments are collected. As with the prepayment clause, a note without a late charge will be subjected to a greater discount.

7. **Seasoned Notes:** A so-called "green" second is one which is so new the borrower has not had a chance to prove his reliability in making prompt payments. A green loan may also lack enough protective equity, as not enough time has elapsed for the home to increase much in value. This is more often true with purchase money than hard money seconds. Largely because of these reasons a new second will probably face a higher discount in the open market.

On the other side of the coin is what is called a seasoned note. It is a loan with only a year or two to run. This shorter period plus a high discount can make it quite attractive to the investor who prefers to take little or no risk. And as I pointed out before, the actual rate of interest is greater on loans with shorter remaining terms.

8. **Borrower:** A loan to a well qualified borrower with a history of "on-time" repayments will fare much better on the open market than one with a borrower who is on the verge of bankruptcy and is continually late with his payments.

With a seasoned note you should be able to tell how well the borrower has done. With a green note you will want to take a close look at the borrower's pre-loan history. With a green purchase money loan you should find out if the borrower bought by assumption or with new terms. The assumption method could indicate that he bought over his head or maybe paid too much for the property. But if he bought with government or conventional terms then the home should have an accurate appraisal plus the borrower's financial background would have been thoroughly checked.

The lesson here is simple. When buying a note with a questionable borrower you take on a greater potential risk and nuisance. Therefore you must demand a larger discount (perhaps 20 instead of 10 per cent) from the seller.

9. **Security:** The security for your loan is the property which the mortgage or deed of trust pledges to the lender in case of default. To protect your security two things must be kept in mind at all times.

One is the amount of equity in the property. As we have already discussed equity percentages in great detail let's concentrate on the second item. And that is the condition of the property and neighborhood.

Needless to say, a property that is well maintained, only 10 years old and in a nice neighborhood that appreciates in value as well as others in surrounding areas must be given an A rating for security. But most properties don't fall into that mold. A home might need new carpeting plus minor repairs and fresh paint. The cost of this refurbishing could easily come to $5,000—and in that case you would have to deduct $5,000 from the equity position. If you had to foreclose, this $5,000 might be needed to just put the home back into salable condition.

Physical condition is one thing. But also don't overlook the age of the home and the "direction of the neighborhood." Many 50- or 60-year-old homes seem like they were built to last forever. If that's the case—great! But many older homes show their age, so be careful or you might end up with a major overhaul. If you have any doubts, consult a contractor.

"Direction of neighborhood" refers to growth patterns. Is the area improving, remaining static or deteriorating? A deteriorating neighborhood can mean trouble. Look for telltale signs like unkept yards, new commercial or multiple construction and abandoned homes. You should be able to see deterioration but if you have any doubts call one or all of the following: the police department, a Realtor or the city or county planning department.

As a general rule it is a good idea to have your loan broker (or yourself) inspect the property and neighborhood before buying a discounted loan. If you like the loan but not the property or neighborhood, then make sure your discount is big enough to justify the risk.

Those investors with a gambler's instinct like these high risk loans because, with discount and all, they can consistently earn big yields. It can be done, but I would recommend getting a little experience first before entering the high risk market.

10. **Broker's Commission:** A loan broker's commission does not affect your investment yield when you buy a new loan. But it does enter the picture when you buy a discounted note. And rightly so, because he legitimately earns it.

The broker's commission enters the picture in this manner. The loan broker will examine both the note and the property and then offer the seller a discounted price. The offered price will allow for both a commission and an attractive discount for the investor. Thus with a 14 per cent discount, 4 per cent may go to the broker and 10 per cent to the investor.

When buying a discounted second from a broker, be sure and clarify at the onset what percentage is actually yours.

WHERE TO FIND DISCOUNTED SECONDS

Most of your opportunities will be for new loans. But as almost any investor is desirous of increasing his portfolio profits, seconds that can yield 12, 15 or 20 per cent are in great demand.

There are four good ways to locate them. The first two are obvious. Let your loan broker know that you are interested and also inform all the local Realtors. These are your two best sources.

In addition you can place a classified ad in the local newspaper under the appropriate heading. Consider letting it run 30 days if the ad rates are reasonable for the longer period. Your copy could read as follows:

> *Private Party will buy second mortgages at reasonable discount. Cash-out in 48 hours or less. Call — —*

Your last source of locating seconds is a little more complicated. To start with it involves reading your community's legal newspaper— if one is published. In my area it is called the "Contra Costa News-Register." It does not contain news stories or retail advertisements but does print lists of all legal county recordings including divorces, defaults and property transfers. Thus this newspaper is a source for the address and names of all persons who are parties to real estate loans.

What you should do is make a list of each apparent lender that has executed a second. This might be done by looking for the approximate amount of money changing hands in a transaction. It is obvious a large sum would represent a first loan while a $5,000 figure would most likely represent a second.

Although your legal newspaper may report the address of the subject property, it probably will not give the lender's address. If no address is given then you will have to match the name with one in the telephone book and hope you are right.

Once you have a dozen or so names write them a letter offering to purchase their existing second at any time they might want to sell. A certain percentage will come through and you will be dollars ahead.

Five Ways of
Increasing Your Profits

So far I've talked about the basic ins and outs of secondary investing which can lead to better profits than you would find with most other investments.

But for those of you who would rather get rich overnight than to plow along at a steady pace — this chapter delves further into five ideas that just might help you get rich a little faster, but not overnight. You might want to include one or more into your financial "game plan." They are: out of state opportunities; the pyramid approach; discounting for profit; borrowing someone else's money; and the Keogh Plan.

In the first chapter I discussed the necessity of establishing and sticking to a financial goal. This is especially important when planning long-range investments. And seconds certainly can be considered long-range investments. If you want to double your money overnight, then you are reading the wrong book.

But if you are thinking in terms of 10 to 30 years then keep on reading because you are heading in the right direction. Seconds are an investment field that should never return less than 10 per cent yearly and possibly as much as 25 per cent on your investment dollar.

Remember that $10,000 invested at 10 per cent, annually compounded, will return $174,494 in 30 years. But the same amount at only 12 per cent will return $299,599. Thus only a 2 per cent difference in interest will mean $125,105 over a 30-year period.

Just imagine then what could happen if you were able to maintain an average return of 20 per cent for a 30-year period. If you are ready for it, here is the answer — a staggering $2,373,761. Of course, making this amount assumes that you don't spend any money and that you can completely avoid all taxes.

But the moral of the story is well illustrated. Sticking to a well defined long-range goal coupled with the highest interest rates you can get will certainly make you money. A lot more money than your bank will pay!

The balance of this chapter is dedicated to those readers who will develop a long-range "game plan" so that they live their retirement years in comfort and not be dependent upon Uncle Sam's meager social security payments.

OUT OF STATE OPPORTUNITIES

If your home state does not offer a high interest rate or if it uses a mortgage with a long redemption period, then send your money out of state. You will probably find a lot of people already doing so. Check the interest and security device charts on pages 50 and 52.

A good example would be Colorado. In that state you can earn 18 per cent and, according to my sources, most seconds are made at that high percentage. There is only one obvious problem. Colorado is a fairly small state population-wise and there are only so many opportunities. A thousand out of state investors could almost dry up the market.

If you are going to invest out of state, you should consider selecting three loan brokers in three different states. There are a lot to choose from including Utah (unlimited interest rate), Nevada (12 per cent), North Carolina (12 per cent) and Washington (12 per cent). All of these states primarily use the deed of trust.

If you live in a state like Michigan (7 per cent), your only real opportunity is to send your money elsewhere. In time I believe low interest states will realize how much stronger their building and real estate industries would be with a viable secondary money market. But until they change, go West or South or East—but go where the action is heavy and the returns are high.

THE PYRAMID APPROACH

The second and most basic approach to making money with seconds is that of pyramiding. With this approach you can start with $2,000 or $10,000 or $100,000. But whether you start out small or large, the principles are the same. The object is to "turn over" your money as fast as possible without spending any until you have arrived at the point in your goal when it is "okay" to spend.

To pyramid effectively you will want to always obtain the highest possible interest rates. You will also want to keep your money in circulation.

Thus you must take the best loans available. One time this might mean a 10 per cent note and another time it might be a discounted note with a yield of 15 per cent. The important thing is to keep your money in circulation at high interest rates. What money is not in circulation, but waiting for a new loan, should be earning at least 4½ to 5 per cent in a local bank or savings and loan association.

When pyramiding you will receive your best results with loans that are fully amortized or have a high pay-back. This is because you get more money back quickly which in turn you can put out again at 10 per cent or better.

When you can average a 12 per cent yield, then your original investment will double in six years and triple in nine years. Soon your only problem will be taxes eating away at your profits.

And to some extent there is an answer to the tax problem. In my first book *The Monopoly Game,* the how to book of making big money with rental homes," I explain how an investor can make excellent profit (often up to 100 per cent) by buying, renting and then later selling or refinancing single family homes. Admittedly, a lot more work and risk is involved with rental homes than seconds. But because of potentially high returns plus the tax shelter advantage, many people favor this investment.

Both forms of investment are compatible partners. For instance, four or five rental properties can bring an investor upwards to $8,000 in tax shelter. And if you are in the 36 per cent tax bracket (married taxpayers earning a taxable income of $24,000 to $28,000) then this $8,000 deduction will save you 36 per cent or $2,880. That's $2,880 that Uncle Sam won't get or the equivalent of $8,000 in yearly "second" profit that can be protected by offsetting the gain against the rental tax loss.

THE OTHER SIDE OF THE COIN

Just as owning a few rental properties can help the "second" investor get started, seconds can be a big help to the real property investor after he reaches his rainbow.

In *The Monopoly Game* I outlined an 11-year plan where a typical investor could start with $3,000 or $4,000 and end up with a portfolio of eight homes worth approximately $300,000. These figures are based on home appreciation levels of 10 per cent annually. Perhaps a conservative figure even, considering homes in the West increased 16.9 per cent from September 1975 thru September 1976.

But for those real property investors who are reaching retirement age, or shall we say travel years, the management of eight or more homes can become a problem. Many will now be concerned with liquidation of assets without giving most of their money to Uncle Sam.

But there is a partial answer — it's using the remaining properties to shield as much income as possible while transferring investments from real property to seconds.

With eight properties, for instance, it would be an eight-year program. Each year the investor would sell only one home so as not to trigger high capital gains taxes. The money left over after sales expenses and taxes would be put into seconds. This should be as much as $30,000 the first year and up to $60,000 the last years.

DISCOUNTING FOR PROFIT

As I pointed out in Chapter I, if the Consumer Price Index continues at anything close to its present percentage rate of 6.8, then a $40,000 income won't look very attractive in 30 years, let alone 20. That is because today's $15,000 salary will need to be $86,000 in 30 years just to keep pace.

Because of inflation, you might give serious consideration to the third way of making big profits with seconds. And that is buying seconds at discount. Not just simply a discount that will bring a low interest rate up to par, but a figure that will increase your true yield to 20 or even 30 per cent.

A careful selection of high yield seconds is possible. If half of your portfolio returns 12 per cent and the other half, consisting of well chosen discounted notes, returns an average yield of 20 per cent, then your effective interest profit will be 16 per cent.

The following partial mortgage yield tables will illustrate the discount percentage necessary to realize specific yields.

ORIGINAL INTEREST RATE
8%—DUE IN THREE YEARS

MONTHLY PAYBACK	10% yield	12% yield	14% yield	16% yield	18% yield	20% yield	24% yield
1%	4.86	9.44	13.78	17.87	21.74	25.39	32.11
1½%	4.39	8.56	12.50	16.23	19.76	23.12	29.30
2%	3.93	7.67	11.22	14.59	17.79	20.84	26.50

To compute a 20 per cent return on a loan with a 1½ per cent monthly pay-back (due in three years), start with the pay-back column at the left and read to the right until you reach 23.12 beneath the 20 per cent yield column. Thus to earn a 20 per cent yield you would need to discount the note by 23.12 per cent.

ORIGINAL INTEREST RATE
10%—DUE IN FIVE YEARS

MONTHLY PAYBACK	14% yield	16% yield	18% yield	20% yield	24% yield	28% yield	32% yield
1%	13.60	19.54	24.97	29.95	38.69	46.06	52.28
1½%	11.41	16.47	21.13	25.44	33.11	39.70	45.37
2%	9.23	13.39	17.29	20.93	27.54	33.35	38.47

This chart shows that a 10 per cent note with a 2 per cent pay-back purchased at a one-third discount will yield approximately 28 per cent. You can see that it doesn't take a huge discount to significantly increase your yield.

The preceding tables are just a small part of the mortgage yield (discount percentages) tables contained in the Realty Bluebook. I strongly recommend it for the bargain-hunting investor who is willing to tackle the extra risks involved with buying high yield discounted notes. See page 83 for more details about the book.

While it is generally true that your risks increase with the size of the discount, it is not always the case. The most commonly discounted loans are purchase money. And many property sellers that carry back a purchase money loan have no intentions of keeping them. They go on the market as soon as possible. A fair percentage of these purchase money loans are not only properly drawn but will have the highest interest rates and sufficient equity.

As it is the general practice of the secondary market, the seller of a purchase money loan will be compelled to sell at a discount. And just a 10 per cent discount can add between 4 and 6 per cent to an investor's yield.

While any investor can benefit from higher yields produced by discounting, I feel that this method can be of prime importance to the person who is already in retirement. He does not have time left to set a 20- or 30-year goal. And he may need all the income he can get for current living expenses. If this is your situation, then the high yields produced by discounting may be the right investment answer.

A word of warning, however. It is not always easy to locate seconds that sell for large discounts. You might have to wait months before you can find one to your liking. Buying discounted seconds is best left to those with either a great deal of patience or with enough desire to do the legwork necessary to find them.

BORROWING SOMEONE ELSE'S MONEY

An often difficult but basic approach to the subject of earning money is to borrow someone else's and then re-invest it for a higher return. If you could borrow all the money you wanted at 5 per cent and then put it out at 10 per cent, it is obvious that you would soon become a very rich person.

Because we are taught by age 10 not to believe in fairy tales, most of us don't even consider this basic approach. But I have news for you! This method can work for most people right now. If you can borrow at 9 or 10 per cent and invest consistently at 13 or 14 per cent, then you are on the road to making a bundle.

I just described two methods of earning far better than average yields. One was to invest in a high interest state and the second was to buy high yield discounted notes. Both methods should return a minimum of 12 per cent, and with the discounting approach you could realize an average return between 14 and 20 per cent.

Now if you could borrow money at 9 per cent and re-invest it at say just 14 per cent, you would be using 100 per cent leverage and earning a clear profit of 5 per cent.

The next logical question, of course, is where do you get the money? Here are some answers to that question:

1. **Your Residence:** If you are a homeowner with sufficient equity, you could refinance your property. At this writing the interest rates for a new first mortgage would run between 8½ and 9½ per cent. The refinancing costs, spread over the term of the new loan, would bring the effective cost up another ½ to 1 per cent.

Not only will refinancing release additional investment funds, but it will increase your tax depreciation base (with rental properties only) and your interest deductions (for your residence and rental property) and thus give you additional tax shelter and savings.

Refinancing is not for everyone, however. Make sure that you can readily obtain the second loans you want before you refinance. Refinance only when interest rates are low. And don't refinance if your age, employment projections or health considerations leave you with any doubts.

2. **Life Insurance:** It just might be that you have a whole life insurance policy with sufficient equity for a loan. Many life insurance companies will lend against your policy equity at rates as low as 6 to 8 per cent.

3. **Friends or Relatives:** Throughout the United States there are literally millions of people who are "storing" billions of dollars in banks and savings institutions. To many of these people their savings account is an investment.

Now you just might have an uncle or a cousin who would be more than happy to lend you $10,000 at 9 per cent rather than continue to accept 6 to 8 per cent on time certificates.

But be careful with friends or relatives. It can be touchy! For some people this source should be scratched. If you do get a loan, however, be fair. You might consider adding your uncle's name to the note and security device as a co-borrower. In this way you can offer substantial security for your mutually benefiting arrangement.

4. **Bank Loan:** A bank loan is a long shot, but there could come a time when it would be practical.

For instance, an opportunity could come along to buy a $10,000, 10 per cent note for $7,500 or a 25 per cent discount. This could give you a yield of approximately 18 to 21 per cent, depending upon the monthly pay-back and duration. Now if you didn't have the liquid cash but had good enough credit and security for a $7,500 bank loan, you could make the deal if the terms were favorable.

When interest rates are generally low you will usually find the banks with a low prime rate. This could mean a rate to you of between 12 and 14 per cent. Trading 14 for 21 per cent can make sense.

But when interest and prime rates are high, your loan costs could range from 15 to 20 per cent. So with the higher rates borrowing from the bank probably won't make much dollar sense.

I recommend that you prepare today for tomorrow. See your banker and find out what interest rates you would be charged in both good and bad times. Find out if your credit and collateral are solid enough for a bank loan. Simply find out if you could possibly receive a loan some time in the future if a "hot" buy comes along.

THE KEOGH PLAN

If you are self-employed or a professional, you can probably qualify for what is known as the Keogh Plan. And this plan can be used in conjunction with your junior lien portfolio.

Because the Keogh is basically a tax shelter-retirement plan, you cannot withdraw funds without penalty until you are 59½. Your contributions, up to 15 per cent of your earnings or $7,500 (whichever is less), are tax free until they are distributed to you on your retirement.

So for some investors, the Keogh Plan is the way to accumulate the large sums of money talked about earlier in the book. The government will help keep your hands out of the cookie jar.

Many existing plans are offered. All you need to do is sign up. But through investigation I have found that very few of the existing plans deal with secondary financing. Most offer what I consider to be low yielding stocks, mutual funds, life insurance policies or time certificate accounts.

If you cannot find an existing plan that deals with secondary loans, then you can set one up. But there are some difficulties so you should get some help in doing so.

Your Keogh Plan must be overseen by what IRS calls trusts or custodial accounts. These duties are performed by trust companies and many banks. There are costs, however, often as much as $150 to $350 per year. But that's not bad when you consider what $4,000 per year for 30 years can bring when invested at 12 or 15 per cent.

Conclusion

The purpose of this book is to acquaint the public with the opportunities to increase income via second mortgages and deeds of trust.

The opportunities are real. I know of many people who supplement their income in this way. I am aware of others who have retired in relative comfort by using the principles discussed in this book.

There are no dark and hidden secrets. Just basic facts which when mastered can lead to a better income.

If you decide to invest in seconds you have two clear choices. You can find a reliable loan broker and entrust your investment program to him. Or you can do it yourself.

If you decide to basically do it on your own, then I caution you to make sure you understand the basic principles. And go one step beyond this book! Discover what the laws are in the state where you plan to invest. Laws and customs vary just enough so that you could run into problems if you don't thoroughly acquaint yourself with them.

I sincerely hope that you have found "How to Grow a Money-tree" a little bit magical in demonstrating ways you can "grow" more dollars in the years ahead.

About The Author

A native of Oakland, California, David Glubetich was graduated from San Jose State College in 1961 with a degree in journalism—public relations. He went into real estate in 1965, after two years as Executive Manager of the Oakland Junior Chamber of Commerce and two years as manager of the Pleasant Hill Chamber of Commerce.

In 1969 he purchased Wells Realty, a general brokerage firm, in Pleasant Hill, California. He continues to own and operate the company, which is now affiliated with Electronic Realty Associates.

His first book, "The Monopoly Game," was self-published in 1975. Over 30,000 copies are now in print.

INFLATION FACTOR TABLE
Average Annual Rate of Inflation Expected

	3.0%	3.5%	4.0%	4.5%	5.0%	5.5%	6.0%	6.5%	7.0%	7.5%
1	1.030	1.035	1.040	1.045	1.050	1.055	1.060	1.065	1.070	1.075
2	1.060	1.071	1.081	1.092	1.102	1.113	1.123	1.134	1.144	1.155
3	1.092	1.108	1.124	1.141	1.157	1.174	1.191	1.207	1.225	1.242
4	1.125	1.147	1.169	1.192	1.215	1.238	1.262	1.286	1.310	1.335
5	1.159	1.187	1.216	1.246	1.276	1.306	1.338	1.370	1.402	1.435
6	1.194	1.229	1.265	1.302	1.340	1.378	1.418	1.459	1.500	1.543
7	1.229	1.272	1.315	1.360	1.407	1.454	1.503	1.553	1.605	1.659
8	1.266	1.316	1.368	1.422	1.477	1.534	1.593	1.654	1.718	1.783
9	1.304	1.362	1.423	1.468	1.551	1.619	1.689	1.762	1.838	1.917
10	1.343	1.410	1.480	1.552	1.628	1.708	1.790	1.877	1.967	2.061
11	1.384	1.459	1.539	1.622	1.710	1.802	1.898	1.999	2.104	2.215
12	1.425	1.511	1.601	1.695	1.795	1.901	2.012	2.129	2.252	2.381
13	1.468	1.563	1.665	1.772	1.885	2.005	2.132	2.267	2.409	2.560
14	1.512	1.618	1.731	1.851	1.979	2.116	2.260	2.414	2.578	2.752
15	1.557	1.675	1.800	1.935	2.078	2.232	2.396	2.571	2.759	2.958
16	1.604	1.733	1.872	2.022	2.182	2.355	2.540	2.739	2.952	3.180
17	1.652	1.794	1.947	2.113	2.292	2.383	2.692	2.917	3.158	3.419
18	1.702	1.857	2.025	2.208	2.406	2.621	2.854	3.106	3.379	3.675
19	1.753	1.922	2.106	2.307	2.526	2.765	3.025	3.308	3.616	3.951
20	1.806	1.989	2.191	2.411	2.653	2.917	3.207	3.523	3.869	4.247
21	1.860	2.059	2.278	2.520	2.785	3.078	3.399	3.752	4.140	4.566
22	1.916	2.131	2.369	2.633	2.925	3.237	3.603	3.996	4.430	4.908
23	1.973	2.206	2.464	2.752	3.071	3.426	3.819	4.256	4.740	5.277
24	2.032	2.283	2.563	2.876	3.225	3.614	4.048	4.533	5.072	5.672
25	2.093	2.363	2.665	3.005	3.386	3.813	4.291	4.827	5.427	6.098
26	2.156	2.445	2.772	3.140	3.555	4.023	4.549	5.141	5.807	6.555
27	2.221	2.531	2.883	3.282	3.733	4.244	4.822	5.475	6.213	7.047
28	2.287	2.620	2.998	3.429	3.920	4.477	5.111	5.831	6.648	7.575
29	2.356	2.711	3.118	3.584	4.116	4.724	5.418	6.210	7.114	8.144
30	2.427	2.806	3.243	3.745	4.321	4.983	5.743	6.614	7.612	8.754
31	2.500	2.905	3.373	3.913	4.538	5.258	6.088	7.044	8.145	9.411
32	2.575	3.006	3.508	4.089	4.764	5.547	6.453	7.502	8.715	10.117
33	2.652	3.111	3.648	4.274	5.003	5.852	6.830	7.989	9.325	10.876
34	2.731	3.220	3.794	4.466	5.253	6.174	7.251	8.509	9.978	11.691
35	2.813	3.333	3.946	4.667	5.516	6.513	7.868	9.062	10.676	12.568
36	2.898	3.450	4.103	4.877	5.791	6.872	8.147	9.651	11.423	13.511
37	2.985	3.571	4.268	5.096	6.081	7.250	8.636	10.278	12.223	14.524
38	3.074	3.696	4.458	5.326	6.385	7.648	9.154	10.946	13.079	15.614
39	3.167	3.825	4.616	5.565	6.704	8.069	9.703	11.658	13.994	16.785
40	3.262	3.959	4.801	5.816	7.039	8.513	10.285	12.416	14.974	18.044

98

DO NOT DESTROY THIS NOTE: When paid, this note and the Deed of Trust must be surrendered to the First American Title Insurance Company with request for reconveyance.

INSTALLMENT NOTE

(INTEREST INCLUDED)

(This note contains an acceleration clause)

$_____   _____, California, _____

In installments and at the times hereinafter stated, for value received _____

promise_____ to pay to

or order, at

the principal sum of _____ Dollars,

with interest from _____ on the amounts of principal remaining from time to time

unpaid, until said principal sum is paid, at the rate of _____ per cent, per annum. Principal and interest due

in monthly installments of _____ Dollars,

($_____), or more on the _____ day of each and every month, beginning on the _____ day

of _____ 19____

and continuing until said principal sum and the interest thereon has been fully paid. AT ANY TIME, THE PRIVILEGE IS RESERVED TO PAY MORE THAN THE SUM DUE. Each payment shall be credited first, on the interest then due; and the remainder on the principal sum; and interest shall thereupon cease upon the amount so credited on the said principal sum. Should default be made in the payment of any of said installments when due, then the whole sum of principal and interest shall become immediately due and payable at the option of the holder of this note.

If the trustor shall sell, convey or alienate said property, or any part thereof, or any interest therein, or shall be divested of his title or any interest therein in any manner or way, whether voluntarily or involuntarily, without the written consent of the beneficiary being first had and obtained beneficiary shall have the right, at its option, to declare any indebtedness or obligations secured hereby, irrespective of the maturity date specified in any note evidencing the same, immediately due and payable.

Should suit be commenced to collect this note or any portion thereof, such sum as the Court may deem reasonable shall be added hereto as attorney's fees. Principal and interest payable in lawful money of the United States of America. This note is secured by a certain DEED OF TRUST to the FIRST AMERICAN TITLE INSURANCE COMPANY, a California corporation, as TRUSTEE.

1076 (4/72)

INSTALLMENT NOTE 99

Order No._____

Escrow No._____

Loan No._____

————————SPACE ABOVE THIS LINE FOR RECORDER'S USE————————

Request For Notice Under Section 2924b Civil Code

In accordance with Section 2924b, Civil Code, request is hereby made that a copy of any Notice of

Default and a copy of any Notice of Sale under the Deed of Trust recorded as instrument No._____

on _____, 19____, in Book_____, Page_____, Official

Records of_____County, California, and describing land therein as

100

executed by _____, as Trustor,

in which _____ is named as

Beneficiary, and _____, as Trustee,

be mailed to _____,

_____
Number and Street

_____
City and State

STATE OF CALIFORNIA
COUNTY OF _____ } ss.

On _____
before me, the undersigned, a Notary Public in and for said

State, personally appeared _____

_____

_____

known to me to be the person _____ whose name _____
subscribed to the within instrument and acknowledged that
_____ executed the same.

WITNESS my hand and official seal.

Signature _____

_____
Name (Typed or Printed)

FORM 1168

REQUEST FOR NOTICE   101

DEED OF TRUST
WITH POWER OF SALE

FIRST AMERICAN

First American
Title Insurance
Company
TRUSTEE

102

DEED OF TRUST WITH ASSIGNMENT OF RENTS
(This Deed of Trust contains an acceleration clause)

This DEED OF TRUST, made   , between

herein called TRUSTOR,

whose address is

_____   _____   _____
(Number and Street)   (City)   (State)

FIRST AMERICAN TITLE INSURANCE COMPANY, a California corporation, herein called TRUSTEE, and

WITNESSETH: That Trustor grants to Trustee in Trust, with Power of Sale, that property in the

County of

, State of California, described as:

, herein called BENEFICIARY,

If the trustor shall sell, convey or alienate said property, or any part thereof, or any interest therein, or shall be divested of his title or any interest therein in any manner or way, whether voluntarily or involuntarily, without the written consent of the beneficiary being first had and obtained, beneficiary shall have the right, at its option, to declare any indebtedness or obligations secured hereby, irrespective of the maturity date specified in any note evidencing the same, immediately due and payable.

Together with the rents, issues and profits thereof, subject, however, to the right, power and authority hereinafter given to and conferred upon Beneficiary to collect and apply such rents, issues and profits.

For the Purpose of Securing (1) payment of the sum of $ _____ with interest thereon according to the terms of a promissory note or notes of even date herewith made by Trustor, payable to order of Beneficiary, and extensions or renewals thereof, and (2) the performance of each agreement of Trustor incorporated by reference or contained herein (3) Payment of additional sums and interest thereon which may hereafter be loaned to Trustor, or his successors or assigns, when evidenced by a promissory note or notes reciting that they are secured by this Deed of Trust.

To protect the security of this Deed of Trust, and with respect to the property above described, Trustor expressly makes each and all of the agreements, and adopts and agrees to perform and be bound by each and all of the terms and provisions set forth in subdivision A, and it is mutually agreed that each and all of the terms and provisions set forth in subdivision B of the fictitious deed of trust recorded in Orange County August 17, 1964, and in all other counties August 18, 1964, in the book and at the page of Official Records in the office of the county recorder of the county where said property is located, noted below opposite the name of such county, namely:

COUNTY	BOOK	PAGE	COUNTY	BOOK	PAGE	COUNTY	BOOK	PAGE	COUNTY	BOOK	PAGE
Alameda	1288	556	Kings	858	713	Placer	1028	379	Sierra	38	187
Alpine	3	130-31	Lake	437	110	Plumas	166	1307	Siskiyou	506	762
Amador	133	438	Lassen	192	367	Riverside	3778	347	Solano	1287	621
Butte	1330	513	Los Angeles	T-3878	874	Sacramento	5039	124	Sonoma	2067	427
Calaveras	185	338	Madera	911	136	San Benito	300	405	Stanislaus	1970	56
Colusa	323	391	Marin	1849	122	San Bernardino	6213	768	Sutter	655	585
Contra Costa	4684	1	Mariposa	90	453	San Francisco	A-804	596	Tehama	457	183
Del Norte	101	549	Mendocino	667	99	San Joaquin	2855	283	Trinity	108	595
El Dorado	704	635	Merced	1660	753	San Luis Obispo	1311	137	Tulare	2530	108
Fresno	5052	623	Modoc	191	93	San Mateo	4778	175	Tuolumne	177	160
Glenn	469	76	Mono	69	302	Santa Barbara	2065	881	Ventura	2607	237
Humboldt	801	83	Monterey	357	239	Santa Clara	6626	664	Yolo	769	16
Imperial	1189	701	Napa	704	742	Santa Cruz	1638	607	Yuba	398	693
Inyo	165	672	Nevada	363	94	Shasta	800	633			
Kern	3756	690	Orange	7182	18	San Diego SERIES 5 Book 1964, Page 149774					

shall inure to and bind the parties hereto, with respect to the property above described. Said agreements, terms and provisions contained in said subdivision A and B, (identical in all counties, and printed on the reverse side hereof) are by the within reference thereto, incorporated herein and made a part of this Deed of Trust for all purposes as fully as if set forth at length herein, and Beneficiary may charge for a statement regarding the obligation secured hereby, provided the charge therefor does not exceed the maximum allowed by law.

The undersigned Trustor, requests that a copy of any notice of default and any notice of sale hereunder be mailed to him at his address hereinbefore set forth.

Signature of Trustor _____

STATE OF CALIFORNIA }
COUNTY OF } ss.

On _____
before me, the undersigned, a Notary Public in and for said
State, personally appeared _____

known to me to be the person whose name _____
subscribed to the within instrument and acknowledged that
executed the same.

WITNESS my hand and official seal.

Signature _____

(This area for official notarial seal)

1192 (4/72)

D O   N O T   R E C O R D

The following is a copy of Subdivisions A and B of the fictitious Deed of Trust recorded in each county in California as stated in the foregoing Deed of Trust and incorporated by reference in said Deed of Trust as being a part thereof as if set forth at length therein.

A.   To protect the security of this Deed of Trust, Trustor agrees:

(1)   To keep said property in good condition and repair; not to remove or demolish any building thereon; to complete or restore promptly and in good and workmanlike manner any building which may be constructed, damaged or destroyed thereon and to pay when due all claims for labor performed and materials furnished therefor; to comply with all laws affecting said property or requiring any alterations or improvements to be made thereon; not to commit or permit waste thereof; not to commit, suffer or permit any act upon said property in violation of law; to cultivate, irrigate, fertilize, fumigate, prune and do all other acts which from the character or use of said property may be reasonably necessary, the specific enumerations herein not excluding the general.

(2)   To provide, maintain and deliver to Beneficiary fire insurance satisfactory to and with loss payable to Beneficiary. The amount collected under any fire or other insurance policy may be applied by Beneficiary upon any indebtedness secured hereby and in such order as Beneficiary may determine, or at option of Beneficiary the entire amount so collected or any part thereof may be released to Trustor. Such application or release shall not cure or waive any default or notice of default hereunder or invalidate any act done pursuant to such notice.

(3)   To appear in and defend any action or proceeding purporting to affect the security hereof or the rights or powers of Beneficiary or Trustee; and to pay all costs and expenses, including cost of evidence of title and attorney's fees in a reasonable sum, in any such action or proceeding in which Beneficiary or Trustee may appear, and in any suit brought by Beneficiary to foreclose this Deed.

(4)   To pay: at least ten days before delinquency all taxes and assessments affecting said property, including assessments on appurtenant water stock; when due, all incumbrances, charges and liens, with interest, on said property or any part thereof, which appear to be prior or superior hereto; all costs, fees and expenses of this Trust.

Should Trustor fail to make any payment or to do any act as herein provided, then Beneficiary or Trustee, but without obligation so to do and without notice to or demand upon Trustor and without releasing Trustor from any obligation hereof, may: make or do the same in such manner and to such extent as either may deem necessary to protect the security hereof, Beneficiary or Trustee being authorized to enter upon said property for such purposes; appear in and defend any action or proceeding purporting to affect the security hereof or the rights or powers of Beneficiary or Trustee; pay, purchase, contest or compromise any incumbrance, charge or lien which in the judgment of either appears to be prior or superior hereto; and, in exercising any such powers, pay necessary expenses, employ counsel and pay his reasonable fees.

(5)   To pay immediately and without demand all sums so expended by Beneficiary or Trustee, with interest from date of expenditure at the amount allowed by law in effect at the date hereof, and to pay for any statement provided for by law in effect at the date hereof regarding the obligation secured hereby any amount demanded by the Beneficiary not to exceed the maximum allowed by law at the time when said statement is demanded.

B.   It is mutually agreed:

(1)   That any award of damages in connection with any condemnation for public use of or injury to said property or any part thereof is hereby assigned and shall be paid to Beneficiary who may apply or release such moneys received by him in the same manner and with the same effect as above provided for disposition of proceeds of fire or other insurance.

(2)   That by accepting payment of any sum secured hereby after its due date, Beneficiary does not waive his right either to require prompt payment when due of all other sums so secured or to declare default for failure so to pay.

(3)   That at any time or from time to time, without liability therefor and without notice, upon written request of Beneficiary and presentation of this Deed and said note for endorsement, and without affecting the personal liability of any person for payment of the indebtedness secured hereby, Trustee may: reconvey any part of said property; consent to the making of any map or plat thereof; join in granting any easement thereon; or join in any extension agreement or any agreement subordinating the lien or charge hereof.

(4)   That upon written request of beneficiary stating that all sums secured hereby have been paid, and upon surrender of this Deed and said note to Trustee for cancellation and retention or other disposition as Trustee in its sole discretion may choose and upon payment of its fees, Trustee shall reconvey, without warranty, the property then held hereunder. The recitals in such reconveyance of any matters or facts shall be conclusive proof of the truthfulness thereof. The Grantee in such reconveyance may be described as "the person or persons legally entitled thereto."

(5)   That as additional security, Trustor hereby gives to and confers upon Beneficiary the right, power and authority, during the continuance of these Trusts, to collect the rents, issues and profits of said property, reserving unto Trustor the right, prior to any default by Trustor in payment of any indebtedness secured hereby or in performance of any agreement hereunder, to collect and retain such rents, issues and profits as they become due and payable. Upon any such default, Beneficiary may at any time without notice, either in person, by agent, or by a receiver to be appointed by a court, and without regard to the adequacy of any security for the indebtedness hereby secured, enter upon and take possession of said property or any part thereof, in his own name sue for or otherwise collect such rents, issues, and profits, including those past due and unpaid, and apply the same, less costs and expenses of operation and collection, including reasonable attorney's fees, upon any indebtedness secured hereby, and in such order as Beneficiary may determine. The entering upon and taking possession of said property, the collection of such rents, issues and profits and the application thereof as aforesaid, shall not cure or waive any default or notice of default hereunder or invalidate any act done pursuant to such notice.

(6)   That upon default by Trustor in payment of any indebtedness secured hereby or in performance of any agreement hereunder, Beneficiary may declare all sums secured hereby immediately due and payable by delivery to Trustee of written declaration of default and demand for sale and of written notice of default and of election to cause to be sold said property, which notice Trustee shall cause to be filed for record. Beneficiary also shall deposit with Trustee this Deed, said note and all documents evidencing expenditures secured hereby.

After the lapse of such time as may then be required by law following the recordation of said notice of default, and notice of sale having been given as then required by law, Trustee, without demand on Trustor, shall sell said property at the time and place fixed by it in said notice of sale, either as a whole or in separate parcels, and in such order as it may determine, at public auction to the highest bidder for cash in lawful money of the United States, payable at time of sale. Trustee may postpone sale of all or any portion of said property by public announcement at such time and place of sale, and from time to time thereafter may postpone such sale by public announcement at the time fixed by the preceding postponement. Trustee shall deliver to such purchaser its deed conveying the property so sold, but without any covenant or warranty, express or implied. The recitals in such deed of any matters or facts shall be conclusive proof of the truthfulness thereof. Any person, including Trustor, Trustee, or Beneficiary as hereinafter defined, may purchase at such sale.

After deducting all costs, fees and expenses of Trustee and of this Trust, including cost of evidence of title in connection with sale, Trustee shall apply the proceeds of sale to payment of: all sums expended under the terms hereof, not then repaid, with accrued interest at the amount allowed by law in effect at the date hereof; all other sums then secured hereby; and the remainder, if any, to the person or persons legally entitled thereto.

(7)   Beneficiary, or any successor in ownership of any indebtedness secured hereby, may from time to time, by instrument in writing, substitute a successor or successors to any Trustee named herein or acting hereunder, which instrument, executed by the Beneficiary and duly acknowledged and recorded in the office of the recorder of the county or counties where said property is situated, shall be conclusive proof of proper substitution of such successor Trustee or Trustees, who shall, without conveyance from the Trustee predecessor, succeed to all its title, estate, rights, powers and duties. Said instrument must contain the name of the original Trustor, Trustee and Beneficiary hereunder, the book and page where this Deed is recorded and the name and address of the new Trustee.

(8)   That this Deed applies to, inures to the benefit of, and binds all parties hereto, their heirs, legatees, devisees, administrators, executors, successors and assigns. The term Beneficiary shall mean the owner and holder, including pledgees, of the note secured hereby, whether or not named as Beneficiary herein. In this Deed, whenever the context so requires, the masculine gender includes the feminine and/or neuter, and the singular number includes the plural.

(9)   That Trustee accepts this Trust when this Deed, duly executed and acknowledged, is made a public record as provided by law. Trustee is not obligated to notify any party hereto of pending sale under any other Deed of Trust or of any action or proceeding in which Trustor, Beneficiary or Trustee shall be a party unless brought by Trustee.

DO NOT RECORD   REQUEST FOR FULL RECONVEYANCE

TO FIRST AMERICAN TITLE INSURANCE COMPANY, TRUSTEE:

The undersigned is the legal owner and holder of the note or notes, and of all other indebtedness secured by the foregoing Deed of Trust. Said note or notes, together with all other indebtedness secured by said Deed of Trust, have been fully paid and satisfied; and you are hereby requested and directed, on payment to you of any sums owing to you under the terms of said Deed of Trust, to cancel said note or notes above mentioned, and all other evidences of indebtedness secured by said Deed of Trust delivered to you herewith, together with the said Deed of Trust, and to reconvey, without warranty, to the parties designated by the terms of said Deed of Trust, all the estate now held by you under the same.

Dated _____

_____

_____

Please mail Deed of Trust,
Note and Reconveyance to _____

Do not lose or destroy this Deed of Trust OR THE NOTE which it secures. Both must be delivered to the Trustee for cancellation before reconveyance will be made.

106

Order No.
Escrow No.
Loan No.

WHEN RECORDED MAIL TO:

ASSIGNMENT OF DEED OF TRUST

FOR VALUE RECEIVED, the undersigned grants, assigns and transfers to:

all beneficial interest under that certain Deed of Trust dated

executed by   , Trustor,

to   , Trustee

and recorded   , as document No.

of Official Records in the office of the County Recorder of

describing land therein as: , in Book   , Page   ,

County, California,

108

TOGETHER with the note or notes therein described or referred to, the money due and to become due thereon with interest, and all rights accrued or to accrue under said Deed of Trust.

Dated _____

STATE OF CALIFORNIA }
COUNTY OF _____ } ss.

On _____

before me, the undersigned, a Notary Public in and for said State, personally appeared _____

_____ known to me to be the person _____ whose name _____ subscribed to the within instrument and acknowledged that _____ executed the same.

WITNESS my hand and official seal.

Signature _____

(This area for official notarial seal)

ASSIGNMENT OF DEED OF TRUST 109

1064 (6/73)

FULL RELEASE OF MORTGAGE

IN CONSIDERATION of the payment of the debt secured by the Mortgage executed:

By _____

To _____

recorded in the office of the County Recorder of _____ County, Arizona, on _____

In Docket _____, at page _____ thereof, said mortgage, together with the debt thereby

secured, is fully paid, satisfied and discharged.

WITNESS _____ hand _____ and seal _____ this _____ day of _____, 19_____

STATE OF ARIZONA
County of _____ } ss.

This instrument was acknowledged before me this _____ day of _____, 19 _____

by _____

_____
Notary Public.

My commission expires _____

Realty Mortgage

KNOW ALL MEN That

of Maricopa County, Arizona, hereinafter referred to as MORTGAGOR, in consideration of

DOLLARS,

to him in hand paid by

hereinafter called Mortgagee,

the receipt whereof is hereby acknowledged, does hereby grant, bargain, sell and convey unto the said

Mortgagee, his heirs and assigns, forever, the following described premises and property, lying and being in

the County of   and State of Arizona, known and described as follows,

to-wit:

112

Together with all buildings and improvements now or hereafter erected thereon and all heating, plumbing, lighting, cooling, air conditioning, and fire prevention fixtures and equipment now or hereafter attached to or used in connection with the premises herein described, together with all and singular the tenements, hereditaments and appurtenances, privileges, water and water rights, pipes, flumes and ditches and the water flowing through the same thereunto belonging or in anywise appertaining, and the reversions, remainders, rents, issues and profits thereof.

TO HAVE AND TO HOLD the same unto the Mortgagee, his heirs and assigns, forever.

And the said Mortgagor hereby covenants and warrants that he is well and truly seized of a good and perfect title in fee simple to the premises above conveyed and has good right and lawful authority to convey the same to the Mortgagee, his heirs and assigns, and that the title hereby conveyed is free, clear and unincumbered; and that he will forever warrant and defend the same to the Mortgagee, his heirs and assigns, against all claims whatsoever.

Provided always, and these presents are upon the express condition that if the Mortgagor shall pay or cause to be paid to the Mortgagee the just and full sum of

Dollars,

with interest thereon, according to the conditions of   certain promissory note   , of even date herewith, executed by the Mortgagor to the Mortgagee, and shall moreover pay annually to the proper officers all taxes and assessments which shall be assessed upon said real estate and any improvements thereon or upon the within described note or this mortgage, and deliver receipts therefor to the Mortgagee on or before the date when such taxes and assessments shall become delinquent, and insure and keep insured the buildings upon said premises in insurance companies designated by the Mortgagee in the sum of at least

Dollars,

with such insurance made payable to the Mortgagee as his interest may appear, and do and perform all the other things herein required to be done and performed, then these presents shall be null and void; and on default in the payment of said taxes or assessments, or premiums for insurance aforesaid, the Mortgagee may pay the same, and such payments, if made, shall be added to the amount of said note and bear interest at the same rate and be secured by these presents. In case of the non-payment of any sum or sums of money, either principal, interest, taxes, assessments, or premiums for insurance, herein mentioned or secured, at the time or times when the same shall become due and payable, agreeable to the conditions of said note or these presents, or in case of the failure of the Mortgagor to keep and perform any other agreement, stipulation, covenant or condition herein mentioned, then and in such case the whole principal sum of said note shall, at the option of the Mortgagee, be deemed to have become immediately due, and the same, with all other costs and charges, each and all with interest at the highest legal rate allowable shall thereupon be collectible by a suit at law or by foreclosure of this mortgage in the same manner as if the whole of said principal sum had been made payable when any such failure shall occur as aforesaid.

The Mortgagor will take reasonable care of the mortgaged premises and the buildings and other improvements thereon, and will maintain the same in good repair and condition as at the original date of this mortgage, ordinary depreciation excepted; and he will commit or permit no waste, and do no act which will unduly impair or depreciate the value of the property as security; and upon any violation of these stipulations upon the part of the Mortgagor, the said note shall become due and payable at once, at the option of the Mortgagee, and this mortgage may thereupon be foreclosed.

In any action to foreclose this mortgage a receiver shall, upon the application of the plaintiff in such action and without notice to the defendants, be appointed by the court to take charge of said property, to manage and carry on the same and to receive and collect the rents, issues and profits thereof and to apply the same to the payment of said note and interest, taxes and other charges, including his own compensation, which may be due or become due during the pendency of the action and until sale be finally made and Sheriff's deed made and delivered hereunder.

In case complaint is filed for the foreclosure of this mortgage, Mortgagor hereby covenants and agrees that he will pay to the Mortgagee, in addition to the expenses and costs of the foreclosure suit, reasonable amount found due, as attorney's fees, and the amount paid by Mortgagee for a title search in preparing such suit, to be included in and become a part of the settlement, if one be made before judgment, or of the judgment, as the case may be, and be a lien upon said premises and be secured by this mortgage.

All the promises and covenants of the Mortgagor shall be binding upon the Mortgagor, his heirs, executors, administrators, successors and assigns, and every stipulation, covenant and agreement herein contained in favor of the Mortgagee shall apply to and inure to the benefit of said Mortgagee, his heirs and assigns.

Wherever the context requires, the singular as herein used shall be deemed to include the plural, and the masculine gender, the feminine and neuter.

IN WITNESS WHEREOF, the Mortgagor ha   hereunto set   hand

this   day of   , A. D., 19

_____

_____

_____

STATE OF ARIZONA
County of ⎰ ss.

This instrument was acknowledged before me this   day of   19 by

My commission will expire _____
                                                    Notary Public.

STATE OF ARIZONA }
County of   } ss.

This instrument was acknowledged before me this _____ day of _____ 19____

by

My commission will expire _____
                                                    Notary Public.

STATE OF ARIZONA, County of Maricopa; ss.
I do hereby certify that the within instrument was filed and recorded at request of _____
_____ on _____ at _____ M., Docket _____
Page _____, Records of Maricopa County, Arizona.
Witness my hand and official seal the day and year firss above written.

                              By _____, County Recorder,
                                                        _____ Deputy.

ATI. 6292 (rev 10/70)

FURNISHED THROUGH COURTESY OF ARIZONA TITLE INSURANCE AND TRUST COMPANY